1964

THE LION OF ARLES

L'essentiel est d'avoir la foi. C'est de croire en l'etoile
qui a si bien guidé notre barque jusqu'ici

MISTRAL

The Lion of Arles

A PORTRAIT OF MISTRAL
AND HIS CIRCLE

by Tudor Edwards

FORDHAM UNIVERSITY PRESS • NEW YORK

Contents

Preface

IT WAS Christmas of 1958 and the writer was in Provence. On the Feast of Saint Stephen (when Provence honors Saint Estève the martyr) or Boxing Day (though the French equivalent, *le Jour des Etrennes*, falls on January 1) I visited Maillane, where I was hospitably received by Monsieur Frédéric Mistral *neveu* and his gracious wife. Since it was a breach of good manners to call immediately after lunch on such a day (though it was unavoidable), my host and hostess were extraordinarily kind, especially since Monsieur Mistral, who as he crossed the garden in his black wide-brimmed hat and muffler reminded me not a little of his illustrious uncle, was suffering from a slight chill and was also being treated for rheumatism at the thermal baths in Aix. It was, then, a great privilege to see the family portraits, the figures of Mirèio, the sculptured bust of an Arlésienne by Contini of Carpentras and a host of Mistralian 'relics,' and to learn, over the coffee and the cognac, of the great celebrations that were to be held in the following year throughout the Midi in honor of the centenary of *Mirèio.*

Monsieur Mistral, who since 1941 has been *Capoulié* of the Félibrige, is the author of the penetrating *Gloses sur Maillane et Mistral* (Paris, 1930) and *Aspects of Mistral* (Marseilles, 1931). He is also the inheritor of the work of Mistral and the guardian of Mistral's as yet unpublished correspondence and other writings.

"Everybody is writing books on Mistral!" exclaimed Mistral *neveu*. It is true that there is an enormous bulk of literature on the subject, but it is almost entirely confined to the French and Provençal languages, while the few works available in English make little or no attempt to portray the hierarchy surrounding the Poet. Since my own sources are indicated in the text, I have considered a bibliography unnecessary. All translations, except where otherwise stated, are my own. My thanks are due to Monsieur Frederic Mistral *neveu* for permission to quote from Mistral's works, to Messrs. Faber and Faber Ltd. for permission to quote from Roy Campbell's poem, *Horses of the Camargue*, and to Messrs. Hollis and Carter Ltd. for permission to quote from Roy Campbell's *Light on a Dark Horse*.

TUDOR EDWARDS

Stanton,
Broadway,
England.

THE LION OF ARLES

BOOK ONE

The Empire of the Sun

Au grand flambeau
S'allument les audaces
Et nous fondions dans l'Espace
L'empire du soleil.

SONG OF THE FÉLIBRIGE

Il y a une vertu dans le soleil.

LAMARTINE

Fai lusi toun blound calèu!
Coucho l'oumbro emai li flèu!
Lèu! lèu! lèu!
Fai te vèire, bèu soulèu!

HYMN TO THE SUN

The sun makes me sing.

MISTRAL

CHAPTER 1

A Farmhouse in Provence

I N F RANCE the year 1830 was a year of revolt. The infamous Talleyrand's foreboding that the kingdom of Charles X would be short-lived (expressed with his usual coarse sentiments as he gazed on the corpse of Louis XVIII in 1824 and said "I smell corruption here") proved right. For, despite his bid to restore the privileges of the old regime and his concessions to the Church, Charles was an unpopular monarch. The Paris Revolution of July 26 sent him tottering, and by the end of August the Duke of Orléans, Louis Philippe, was on the throne as the self-styled Emperor Napoleon II. The Bourbon dynasty was ended.

But down in the Midi where the cigalas trilled and the lizards darted from the sage-green shrub and scented bush and the *scarabée d'or* with its intaglio design of gold and bronze upon its shell-like back became airborne—down there these things seemed to matter comparatively little. The turmoil of the capital seemed as remote as a dream. The vast cypress-pointed sky of Provence hung over a land deep in lavender and thyme, with gnarled fig and olive trees with their weary look of eternity, and the vines staked low upon the earth, all stippled by the burning southern sun and the cold mistral wind, *Madame de Bourgogne,* that hurtled down the Rhône.

North of the white and grotesque range of the rocky Alpilles, in the richly-cultivated lowlands between Avignon and Saint Rémy, the little commune of Maillane went quietly about its business. It was, and is, a village of a few rambling streets of stuccoed houses in soft pastel-colored shades. On the main *place* or village square stood the little belfried church with its modest yet urbane classical façade masking a medieval fabric; it was dedicated, strangely, to St. Agatha, a martyred virgin of Catania in Sicily, where she was still invoked against the eruptions of the volcano Etna, as in Maillane she was invoked against thunder and lightning and fire. Nearby stood the characteristic pylon-like calvary of latticed ironwork. On an even tinier *place* behind the church stood the Cafe dóu Souleu (Cafe of the Sun), with two immense plane trees growing through the verandah roof which overhung the pavement. On the edge of the village the wheel of a water mill turned sluggishly, and a stream flowed beside the road to Saint Rémy, flashing past hedgerows of white hawthorns and plane trees and, in the fields, the vegetables and fruits between the sheltering palisades of reeds. It was a village as fresh and radiant as May, and indeed it was the month of May, *Maiano*, that gave it its name.

Here, on the edge of the village, beside the road to Saint Rémy, in the Mas dóu Juge, or House of the Judge, the long low whitewashed farmhouse with its rose-colored tiles, the Mistral household was awaiting the birth of a child.

François Mistral was a *ménager*, or a well-to-do peasant proprietor-farmer. Provence, almost unique among the provinces of France, was a country of little estates, essentially a country of domestic cultivation by individual families, and in the country about Arles the *ménagers* were a class apart, a kind of aristocracy between the peasants and the bourgeoisie. Thus old François Mistral was fairly well-set-up. He had four pairs of beasts of draught, several carters under a head carter, several ploughmen, a herds-man, a shepherd, and a house servant, in addition to a substantial amount of casual labor, the journeyman and the *gavots* from the mountains, both men and girls, hired by the month or by the day, who came down to assist in the silk weaving, the hoeing of the land, the haymaking, the harvest, the *vendange* or grape gather-ing, the sowing and the olive gathering. In fact, however, the Mis-trals—the name has no etymological connection with the violent wind but derives from the Low Latin *ministralia*, a kind of bailiff—claimed descent from nobility, from lords of Dauphiné, and they held that the fine palazzo-like house in Saint Rémy known as the Hôtel de Mistral de Montdragon was the ancestral family seat.

François Mistral must then have been about fifty-six. Certainly he was some thirty-five years older than his wife Delaide, and he had a son and a daughter by an earlier marriage. His second woo-ing was short and swift, and his acceptance by a mere girl says much for his strength and beauty of character. It was in midsum-mer of the previous year that he was helping his laborers to bring in the harvest, when he was surprised to see an attractive young woman among the gleaners. He went up to her and asked who she was. She told him that she was Delaide, daughter of Estève Poulinet, the *maire* of Maillane.

"What!" said Maître Mistral, "the daughter of the mayor goes gleaning?"

Old Poulinet, a spendthrift in all else, apparently refused his six daughters pocket money for finery and such luxuries and told them to go out and earn it. But if it were strange that the daughter of the mayor should be working in the fields, it seems even stran-ger that Mistral had never before met this girl who lived in the same village. However, the encounter in the cornfields was a charming pastorale, and within a few months Ruth had married her Boaz.

5

Barely two months after the July Revolution Delaide Mistral was brought to childbed, and on the feast of Our Lady's Nativity, September 8, she presented François with the autumnal fruit of his second marriage. At the Mas dóu Juge the year was thus not one of revolt but of benediction. Yet strangely (for it could then have had no significance for the Mistral household) it was a year of revolt in another sphere, for it saw the defeat of Classicism by Romanticism, with Victor Hugo as unchallenged leader of the Romantic school. Delaide Mistral could not have foreseen that her newly-born son would one day become a legendary figure hovering between those two movements. Marked respect was indeed shown to the new infant, but this was the homage paid to every newborn boy-child in Provence and it had a deep and ancient Christian significance.

These traditional and symbolic gestures in honor of the male child were made as the young mother wearing the coiffe of Arles lay ceremonially with the infant in her white-curtained, alcoved bed set upon the polished red floor tiles. Four equally young women, also wearing the traditional costume of Arles, now brought their offerings. The first brought him eggs, with the wish *"siegues plen coume un ióu"*—may you be as full as an egg. The second brought him bread, saying *"siegues bon coume lou pan"*—may you be as wholesome as bread. The third brought him salt, saying *"siegues sage coume la sau"*—may you be as good as salt. And the fourth brought him a large old-fashioned matchstick, saying *"siegues die coume uno brouqueto"*—may you be as straight as a matchstick. Such rites were numerous. The churching of the mother, for example, was never held on a Friday or on the 13th of the month. The baptism of the child was often held on the day of its birth, in the absence of the mother, and the bells of Maillane's steepled church rang out only three times for a girl but again and again for a boy.

6

There was some argument over the name to be given to the child. Madame Mistral, like many Provençaux, had an almost superstitious regard for the predictions of Michael Nostradamus, the sixteenth-century Jewish doctor, astrologer, prophet who was born at Saint Rémy, but a few kilometres from the Mas dóu Juge. Such, in fact, was the extent of this regard that her attempt to christen the child 'Nostradamus' was foiled only by the combined protestations of the *curé* and the *maire*, who refused to register it. There seems to have been but one alternative, and that was the name of a boy who had acted as Cupid's messenger for the parents, carrying letters and messages during their courtship. The name was Frederi (Frédéric), and that was the name duly entered in the register.

Mistral *père* no doubt exercised his authority in this little matter of christening his son, for he ruled his rustic kingdom like a patriarch in Genesis or Hesiod. He was a character of immense grandeur, "brought up and educated, like the Provençaux of old, in the Roman tradition." While he may also have been imbued with a touch of that Nostradamus cult which colored his wife's belief, he was a man of profound faith. His son has described how each evening throughout the year the old man would kneel on a chair, with head bared and hands crossed, reading the prayers to the assembled household and farm laborers. In all his life he had read but three books, and these, quite remarkably, were the Bible, *The Imitation of Christ* and *Don Quixote;* moreover, he owned these books and read them constantly and intensively.

The life at the *mas* was a life in close touch with the soil and with elementals, still dominated by the ancient cycle of times and seasons, traditions and beliefs, when even the simplest meals had an almost monastic ritual. At these meals little Frédéric's stepsister and mother served the food and ate away from the table where sat Maître Mistral, the stepbrother and the male laborers,

7

seated according to rank; nor were girls allowed to drink wine. The master of the house was the first to taste the soup, and at the end of the meal the chief carter gave the signal for all to leave the table by closing the blade of his knife.

But it was his mother who taught him to shape the words of his native language, the old *langue d'oc* of the south, which was spoken by the entire household, the village and indeed all the adjoining countryside. It was she who first kindled in him the love of local history and legend and folklore, firing his imagination as she sat turning her spinning wheel in a corner of that great fireplace. Perhaps of somewhat lower social status than her husband and wholly lacking in sophistication, she was yet a woman of cardinal virtues, and the great Lamartine could later acclaim her as "this beautiful Arlésienne, recalling the heroines of the Bible and of the Odyssey." It was certainly she who encouraged her son to scamper up the road on the feast of the Epiphany, popularly called the *Fête des Rois* or Twelfth Night, along with other children of the village, all carrying little gifts of cakes for the kings, figs for the pages and hay for their camels. But always the Three Kings must have gone another way.

"But what road did you take?" she asked the children who had returned woefully.

"The road to Arles," they replied.

"Oh, my poor silly little sheep. The Kings do not come that way. It is from the East that they come—you must take the road to Rome. . ."

Once again the children would run off. But it was no use. The Kings must have gone behind the mountain. So the children would return home again and perhaps sulk that grownups were such story-tellers. Only then did the mother tell them to go into the church—and there they were, the Kings had taken up their abode in the chapel of the Nativity. Caspar had brought his casket of gold, Melchior carried his censer and Balthazar his jar of myrrh;

they wore brilliant cloaks of red, yellow and blue, and surrounded by their pages and the shepherds they saluted the Infant Jesus.

At *la Saint Jean* or Midsummer night, the night of St. John, patron of the harvest, the reapers and gleaners, young and old, would dance the farandole round the blazing log fire. This *feu de Saint Jean* was a solar festival, and the children jumped (and still do) over the symbolic fires to ensure the return of the sun. Then in September, on the Sunday following the feast day of Saint Eloi, patron of farriers and farmers, Maillane had its own ceremony of the *Charrettes de la Saint Eloi*. The parading carts, garnished with foliage and floral canopies, were drawn by as many as sixty horses and mules decorated with rich trappings and with glittering little mirrors, while the drivers were dressed in white. They were followed by pipers and drummers, and as the cavalcade passed the statue of Saint Eloi the horses and carts were blessed by the priest.

On *Toussaint*, the feast of All Saints, there was feting and feasting, but when evening fell the church bell began to toll for the vigil of All Souls, the *jour des morts*, when the villagers entered into communion with their dead. At the evening meal the children were hurried off to bed, taking with them some of the dessert. The children, young Frédéric among them, would place a portion of their spoils at the foot of the bed for the *armeto*, the spirits of those dead who were still in contact with the living and had not yet reached their final resting place. They were told that if they were good on this night the *armeto* would kiss them, but if they were naughty the *armeto* would scratch their feet. In the neighboring towns of Saint Rémy and Arles the priests, carrying the cross, lighted candles and baskets, went from door to door to beg a little part of the meal for the dead, which would be given to the poor. That night in Maillane, as in every village of the Comtat, the land seemed to be dotted with myriads of fireflies as hundreds of candles and lighted lanterns burned on the graves in

9

the local cemetery. The bleached crosses and rococo tombs were garlanded with flowers and hooped with colored beads, and families sat upon the ground praying, telling their rosaries, laughing and crying, keeping company with their dead until the dawn.

Thus the entire liturgical year was celebrated with piety and zeal, for, as Adolphe Dumas put it, "the South was twice Roman —Roman Latin and Roman Catholic." In the country between Arles and Avignon a Protestant was a rare thing. Yet it was at the *mas* that Mistral, as a child, encountered his first Protestant. He was a Vaudois from the north, by name Pierre Juvénal, who every year with his three sons descended to the plain to sell needles and cottons, ribbons and the fat of the marmot. And each night, with his sons, he would pray in a high voice: *Nostre Paire que es els cels.* It was he, said Mistral in later years, who first revealed to him that one should address oneself to God in Provençal.

It was true that there was a breath of the old pagan world about some of these ceremonies, and the more ancient and pre-Christian rites were celebrated with equal gusto. For a child this was too a country of legendary monsters, the Drac who lived on the bed of the Rhône, a reptilian creature strangely as beautiful as he was repulsive, with long green silky hair and webbed hands and feet and the faculty of transforming himself into a human being, and the Tarasque, a spiked and scaly creature breathing fire, who roamed the hills of the Montagnette. There were other creatures like the Chèvre d'Or, the elusive Golden Goat, lonely and fleet of foot, a sort of Blue Bird of Unhappiness, and the Esprit Fantastique, a kind of Puck or Robin Goodfellow, who, so Mistral tells us, was mischievous and up to all manner of tricks, leading all the animals out to drink at night, and sometimes sweeping the kitchen, tripling the eggs from the fowl, seeing to the fire and turning the roast on the spit.

Soon young Frédéric and his playmates were wandering off in search of such intriguing creatures, and as often as not he played truant from the village school. Not infrequently he returned home in disgrace, for he had soiled his blue velvet dress by falling into ditches and streams as he stretched over to pluck flowers.

When the cries of harvest brought the *gavots*, the mountain people in northwestern Provence, swarming down to the lowland farms for work, the Mas dóu Juge was brimming over with people. It was a busy time for Madame Mistral. At seven o'clock in the morning all had a glass of the local wine and a slice of oiled bread with anchovy. At ten they had a hard-boiled egg, a piece of cheese and watered wine. At one o'clock they assembled for a meal of soup and vegetables. At four they had salad and bread rubbed with garlic, and at night they dined off meat or an onion omelette. The wine was always poured by the *capoulié* or chief harvester. Such conditions and treatment might well have been the envy of contemporary laborers in England or for that matter elsewhere in Europe, but Mistral in citing these conditions in his memoirs gives no indication of the monetary reward, and indeed it is probable that payment was largely made in board and lodging. Certainly these rustic colonies seemed to have a greater capacity for work and enjoyment than our own pampered work-shys. Sometimes before the men retired to rest for the night they would sing the ballad called the "Reapers' Grace"; the first part of this was a variation on the first chapter of Genesis, where Adam and *noues-tro Maire Evo* are put into the Garden of Eden, with the prophecy that Adam would die and be buried under palm, cyprus and olive; the second part, livelier, not only celebrated the feast of the olive but was also an expression of goodwill to the master and mistress of the *mas*, each verse ending *Adorem devotoment Jesù eme Mario*. And dominating all there would be Maître Mistral, "a great and beautiful old man, dignified in his speech, kindly to the poor and harsh only to himself." (Mistral's memoirs *Moun Espelido* or *Mes Origines*).

The harvest led quite naturally to the *vendange*, until such time

11

as the phylloxera all but ruined the vines of Provence and the peasant gave up and cultivated cabbages and other vegetables instead.

At night in the large farmhouse kitchen, with its heavy Provençal furniture, the carved *armoires* or cupboards, the characteristic buffet and the essential bread cupboard and baking apparatus, Madame Mistral would turn her spinning wheel, and sitting by the great cowled fireplace her husband would recall the past, even before the Revolution. The young wide-eyed Frédéric would hear the soft ancient tongue of his ancestors, he would hear how his father fought with the Grand Armée at the siege of Figueras, of the horrors of the *Terreur blanche*, of brigandage in the Estérel, and of the terrible one-night frost that blighted Provence in 1819 when the precious olives were almost ruined forever. And next morning the same well-ordered day with its almost-Trappist ritual and regularity would begin again. For Frédéric, virtually untrammelled by school until his ninth year and allowed to run wild on the farm, it must have been an idyllic childhood in an atmosphere of harmony and sanity, nurtured by traditions of immense antiquity and disciplined by Christian precept and practice.

He was no doubt petted and fussed over by both the household and the marauding army of laborers, but, significantly, he was always addressed as "Moussu Frederi." In accordance with strict Provençal custom only the eldest son, Fédéric's stepbrother, had, as a minor, the right to be called "Mistralet," as Frédéric's stepsister was addressed as "Mistraleto." The distinction marked the heir. Mistral *père* and his wife had therefore decided to compensate Frédéric by giving him the best education within their means, with a hope that his upbringing might foster a vocation for the Church. Accordingly, in his ninth year, the boy was placed in a small boarding school in the abandoned abbey of Saint-Michel de Frigolet, two hours away by the farm wagon.

This partly-ruined monastery stood in the thyme- and lavender-scented hills of the Montagnette. Originally built by the medieval Benedictines of Montmajour, between Arles and Les Baux, as a refuge for their malaria-stricken monks, the abbey had lain derelict since the Revolution. Its twelfth-century cloister, refectory and chapter house remained intact, but there were gaps in the church, where the walls were covered with painted demons, the red flames of hell and the combat between the Archangel and the devil. A chapel was embellished with seventeenth-century art woodwork and gilt given by Anne, Empress of Austria, one of many works she carried out to fulfill the vows she made before the birth of her son, Louis XIV. In such a picturesque environment a certain Monsieur Donnat of Cavaillon had set up an eccentric scholastic establishment precariously conducted on a basis of barter. This Donnat would call on all the farmers in a given area and solicit their patronage.

"Ho, monsieur," the farmers would reply, "that sort of thing is all right for the rich, but we are not used to having lectures for our lads; we have only enough for working the land."

"That's all right," Monsieur Donnat would reply, "just make me an annual payment in provisions—so many loads of corn, so many barrels of wine, so many measures of oil."

The establishment seems to have resembled some of the "free discipline" schools flourishing in England today, and all the concomitant evils of the Victorian English public school were absent. Spare the rod and spoil the child was a maxim to which Monsieur Donnat evidently did not subscribe. At once owner and headmaster, he was often absent doing business with the fathers of both existing and prospective pupils, bartering the fathers' trade products or services for the boys' schooling. There were then some forty pupils, and thus freed from supervision both the boys and the meagrely-paid assistants would go in search of the Chèvre d'Or and make sport on the aromatic hills of the Montagnette, those hills in which Daudet's Tartarin of Tarascon went shooting at caps. And the boys would play hide-and-seek in the abandoned church and burrow into gaping sepulchres filled with ancient skulls and bones of monks.

There were other diversions. The patron saint of Graveson, the hamlet where later was built the railway station for Maillane, was Saint Anthime, who, like Saint Gent, another Provençal rain-maker, was invoked during drought. His statue was carried in procession to the Montagnette and then to the abbey church of Frigolet, where the boys would cluster to witness the ceremony. If on the return of the cortege rain had not fallen, the statue was plunged three times into a stream. The prudent and far-seeing peasants also took with them the statue of Saint Aureille, the saint of the wind, who if necessary could make a downpour cease. The school chaplain had been sent to the district by his archbishop to expiate a venial sin. Father Talon, indeed, like old Brother Gaucher in Daudet's story based upon this same abbey of Frigolet, had a taste for the bottle, and when leading the procession of the *Fête-Dieu* (Corpus Christi) in a neighboring village he had scandalized his flock by wobbling as unsteadily as a thistle from one side to another. Certainly he was an unorthodox *abbé*, to say the least of it, and it appears to have been he and he alone who countenanced the strange Rabelaisian ceremony in the chapel of Saint Marcellin at Boulbon at the annual "Pilgrimage of the Bottles." When all had assembled in this chapel, each man carrying a bottle of wine, the abbé intoned with gusto, "My brethren, uncork your bottles, and receive the Benediction in silence." He then hiccuped a blessing upon the wine, and at the Amen each man crossed himself and took a deep draught of the wine, and then the mayor and the abbé clinked glasses on the altar steps.

Despite these not altogether illuminating examples of human

weakness, Frédéric did not lose the ardent belief instilled into him by his family, and at the daily Mass, at five or six o'clock each morning, he prayed (so he recalls in his memoirs) "with a really ardent faith," while he also sang solo at the Elevation.

Frédéric was not visited very often by his parents, but among those visits was one particularly notable one by Maître Mistral during his son's second year at the school. Frédéric had written home to say that he had begun his Latin studies and that he needed some books. Shortly afterwards his father, alone, nearing his three-score-and-ten years, arrived on his mule Babacho. From a large saddlebag the old man produced no less than five dictionaries, more than half dozen Latin tomes, an enormous jar of ink, a fistful of quills and "enough paper to last seven years." "Frederi," he cried, "t'ai adu quàuqui libre em 'un pau de papié" (Frédéric, I've brought you a few books and a little paper).

It is not surprising that this fantastic school was short-lived. The end came suddenly. This institution which prided itself on the cultivation of decorum and religious virtues was shattered one day to learn that the only female servant was with child. Then it was found that she had disappeared. The black cook, who was suspected of having brought about this calamity, also disappeared. To make matters worse Monsieur Donnat himself disappeared (shortly afterwards to die in a sanatorium). Thus abandoned, the assistants packed their belongings and left. For a few days the aged parents of Donnat, entirely alone, made an effort to hold things together, feeding the boys on potatoes. Then, sadly, the frail old mother told them that it was all over. "My children, there is nothing more left to eat; you must go home." In little groups the boys made for their homes, and young Frédéric took the white road back to Maillane.

CHAPTER 2

Sur Le Pont d'Avignon

AVIGNON IN the early 1840's was no longer so filled with convents, chapels and belfries that it could be called, as Rabelais dubbed it, *la ville sonnante*. The bracelet of walls rebuilt on a magnificent scale by the exiled Popes in 1349-70 was picturesque enough, but its stones were crumbling into a stagnant moat and there were gaps and breaches. The Palais des Papes, filthy and neglected, was a barracks. Viollet-le-Duc, the arch-restorer, had not yet arrived. Nor had the present boulevard, the Rue de la République, been driven clean through the old town like a nail from the railway station to the square now called the Place Georges Clemenceau. There was in fact no railway station, for the railway from Paris through Lyons to Marseilles was not completed until 1848, and most travellers from the north sailed down the Rhône. And where beautiful gardens today crown the Rocher des Dom there was then a cemetery.

Yet it was an intriguing town, the town of Petrarch's Laura, the town in which the rustic world danced a *ronde* upon Saint Bénézet's bridge. Down by the Porte de l'Oulle the gypsy caravans came to rest between the sheltering walls and the mighty swift-flowing Rhône, and just inside the gate there flourished a little eighteenth-century theatre with a stone sunrise carved upon it. There were such Baroque palazzo-like houses as the Hôtel de

Montreal, the Hôtel de Crillon, the Hôtel de Vervins and others, all with ample courtyards and façades garnished and scrolled with sculpture. Opposite the medieval Palais des Papes stood the Ecole de Musique, formerly the Papal Mint (for Avignon, with the neighboring Comtat Venaissin, was a Papal State until 1796), bearing the authentic Roman stamp, the Borghese arms, the garlands issuing from the mouths of masks, the dragons and giant eagles. Then there were houses elegant in the eighteenth-century manner, such as that which since 1835 has housed the Musée Calvert, its interior festive with enriched panelling and plasterwork in gilt and cream, with dragons, garlands and musical trophies carved by the *stuccatori*. Cheek by jowl with the churches of Gothic lamentation were exquisite Renaissance churches like the Jesuit church with its opera-box balconies, the almost-rococo chapels of the Penitents, and the even newer churches which were wholly Parisian in inspiration. These last were miniature Panthéons like the domed round chapel of the Saint-Louis hospice and the finer Oratory, an elliptical rotunda with enriched lunettes in the dome, the whole so admirably lighted that it shimmered in a white sea, contrasting sharply with the gloom of medieval Saint Agricol nearby.

Society and the celebrated were finding their way to Avignon in the aftermath spirit of the Grand Tour, braving the violent mistral which screamed through courtyards and bent the plane trees and frayed one's temper. The Brownings, Lady Blessington and Count d'Orsay had been there a little earlier. Prosper Merimée, arriving in 1835, said that he felt he was in a Spanish town, and he observed that Avignon was full of gallants who carried their coats upon one shoulder like a Spanish cloak. Stendhal, arriving two years later, thought that he was in Italy, and he noted that, as on the banks of the Tiber, men worked in the shade and lay down to sleep in the middle of the streets.

17

It was to this erstwhile Papal capital and city of the Troubadours that young Frédéric was now sent to continue his schooling, in a *pensionnat* in the Rue Petramale. Despite the breaking away from his home it was an exciting venture for a thirteen-year-old boy. The first day must have been a revelation, for when he left Maillane in the farm wagon he was accompanied by his mother, his uncle Bénoni, three aunts and several friends, who were going to make a day—and a night—of it. The road to Avignon was invariably crowded with horse-drawn traffic, and the broad Durance had to be crossed by a ferry boat. In Avignon they looked around the town, dined at the Hôtel de la Provence, and went to the little theatre by the Porte de l'Oulle to see a Provençal comedy, Frédéric's first visit to a theatre. The following morning Frédéric was installed in the *pensionnat* of Monsieur Millet.

Monsieur Millet was almost as eccentric as Monsieur Donnat, but he was not as lovable, and Mistral later caricatured him as a gross individual with "the eyes of a pig and the feet of an elephant." He hailed from Caderousse, near Châteauneuf-du-Pape, and his enthusiasm for a poem by the Abbé Favre, *Lou Siege de Cadaroussa*, was such that he punctuated all the Latin lessons with excerpts and illustrations from the poem, interlacing Virgil with Favre. This was all very well and near enough to Frédéric's own heart, but Monsieur Millet had another flair, a more disturbing one. In the interests of economy he served his pupils almost perpetually with boiled carrots. This was too much for Frédéric, who soon suffered from nostalgia for his home. Chancing to read in a newspaper about the Carthusian monastery of Valbonne,[1] more than fifty kilometres to the north of Avignon, he decided to run away and become a monk of the white company of Saint Bruno. He lost no time in setting out, and as he tramped the long road he thought of Saint Gent, whose pattern of holiness inspired him.

1. Now a sanatorium.

But soon he recalled the distress of the saint's mother when her hermit son had run away. He lost heart; he could not, after all, cause his own mother such grief. He must go first to Maillane and tell his parents of his religious vocation, but by the time he reached his home, late at night, his love for his home had completely dissolved this "vocation." He said nothing of the Valbonne episode and merely cried that he was homesick and fed up with "fat old Millet" and his carrots. The next day he was sent back to school, but with a promise that after the holidays he should go to another school.

Frédéric was nearly fifteen when he went to the Collège Royal of Avignon, conducted by Monsieur Dupuy. Here he came under two decisive influences. First he found that he was regarded as something of an oddity because he was not a *Moussu*, a *Franchiman*, for he found himself among people who spoke French and looked to Paris as their capital, people who derided him for his regional accent and for the old *langue d'oc* which he spoke at home. He realized that all he loved most, the language, customs, dress, traditions and legends of his countryside were held to ridicule. The experience was humiliating, "not only for myself," he wrote later, "but for my family and my race." But if it bit into his pride it also strengthened his independence of character and outlook. He swore to restore "the sacrosanct maternal tongue," and he vowed that he would never enter any profession obliging him to use the foreign language.

Even more significant was his meeting with a new master who arrived at the college a year or so later, "a young professor with a fine black beard." Joseph Roumanille was twelve years older than Mistral. Like Mistral he was the son of well-to-do peasants, the eldest of seven children of a gardener of Saint Rémy, the old town but a league from Maillane. Rather remarkably for his station he had received a good education, passing from the local elementary school to the college of Tarascon, where he learned Latin to such effect that he soon made a reputation for translating Virgil and Homer into Provençal. Later he went as assistant master to a school at Nyons, where the headmaster was the poet Charles Dupuy, brother of Monsieur Dupuy. And now he had arrived in Avignon.

It may be said that the Félibrige and the entire Provençal renaissance were born of a single strange encounter in the dim church of Saint Symphorien, the former Carmelite church, heavy with indifferent paintings of the eighteenth century, on the Place des Carmes. The pupils of the school formed part of the choir there, and it was at Vespers one Sunday evening that young Mistral's mind wandered away from the service as he toyed with the idea of translating into Provençal the seven Penitential psalms. Taking up pencil and paper he began with the text *Purge me with hyssop, and I shall be clean; wash me and I shall be whiter than snow*. At that moment Roumanille, who was responsible for discipline, came up and confiscated the paper. If he expected some schoolboy obscenity he must have been astonished by what he read, couched as it was in excellent if straightforward Provençal verse.

Now Roumanille was himself a lyric poet of some talent and delicacy, and, like Mistral, he treasured the native tongue of old Provence. After Vespers he took the boy for a walk on the ramparts, and there he recited some of his own poems. The poems in question were perhaps a little pedestrian, but Frédéric was enthralled, for here for the first time in his experience was a poet who wrote seriously in his own language. It was "a true blossoming of April flowers," he wrote later, "of wild flowers, flowers prophetic of the Félibrean spring which ravished me with delight until I exclaimed to myself, 'Here is the dawn for which my soul was waiting so that it might open to the light.' "

At this time Roumanille in experimenting with Provençal verse was studying the manuscripts of Nicholas Saboly[2] in the Avignon public library. Saboly wrote over sixty carols, songs and poems in Provençal, some of them fantastic, some of them simple and tender, but all having the naive realism which had been in vogue in the Comtat since the Middle Ages. Born at Monteux early in the seventeenth century, Saboly was educated by the Jesuits of Carpentras, ordained at the age of twenty-one, and became organist at Carpentras Cathedral, later moving to Avignon, where he became Master of Music at the church of Saint Pierre. Popularly known as "the Troubadour of Bethlehem" (since he wrote so much in honor of the Nativity), his Christmas carols and such popular songs as *Aqueli mountagno* are still sung by the children of the Midi, and one sees him as a link in the chain which unites Mistral to the troubadours.

Roumanille had begun by writing verses in French, but when one day he was reading some of these to his friends his mother burst into tears because she could not understand the beautiful things her son was saying. Out of a deep filial love Roumanille decided henceforth to write only in his native tongue, and the incident enabled the Félibrige to claim that the Provençal renaissance was "born of a mother's tear." He was already winning recognition as a poet, and for him the handmaidens of poetry were morality and religion. His verse has its limitations but it has qualities of tenderness and joy, and his gift for laughter has caused Jean Ajalbert to see in him a chaste and Christian Rabelais, a family Rabelais. Later he was to gain an even greater reputation as a prose writer and as the virtual founder of the Félibrige, but in these days of Mistral's schooling he was simply one of the pioneers of Provençal verse.

[2]. *Les Nöels de Saboly*, edited by Francois Seguin, was published in Avignon in 1856.

He was, of course, not the first, as young Mistral, now under his tutelage, was to discover. Roumanille recited to him the work of Jean Reboul, the poet-baker of Nîmes, Pierre Bellot, the draper of Marseilles, Pierre Bonnet, the innkeeper of Beaucaire, Jasmin, the poet-hairdresser of Auch, who with his *curé* rebuilt a church by singing his poems for sous in the streets, and Victor Gélu, the baker's son from Marseilles, the fiery red revolutionary with a voice like bronze, who wrote racy and truculent *chansons* in a materialist idiom, and whose belligerent, gesticulating figure is today to be seen carved above a fountain in Marseilles. With Jasmin, whose real name was Jacques Boé, Mistral was already acquainted, having found his poems in a newspaper. Indeed Frédéric sent him a schoolboy's tribute in verse which the older poet ignored, but despite this Mistral, generous as ever, was later to praise Jasmin and to record that he "sang of love better than any woman."

These were the *poétes-ouvriers*, the singers of the people, who prepared the ground for the revival of letters which was to go hand in hand with the rehabilitation of the old language and which was to make the people of the south race conscious. The *langue d'oc* of the Middle Ages and the troubadours had been driven out by the *langue d'oil* of the north which had developed into modern French. It is worth pointing out, however, that Provence was not technically French until 1246, when it was acquired by the family of Anjou, or more strictly 1487, when Charles VIII incorporated it. For centuries after that the old native language still remained on the lips of the people. In 1646, the Archbishop of Arles decreed that his priests must speak Provençal, and two centuries later still, early in the last century (before Mistral's birth) we find Monsiegneur de Mazenod, Bishop of Marseilles, preaching *only* in Provençal. It was in fact only in the latter part of the eighteenth century that the French language spread to the larger towns, and it was not until the process of centralization that followed the Revolution (when Provence lost its ancient rights and privileges) that the use of the French language really became widespread. In Provence numerous dictionaries and grammar manuals were then published, but they were designed not for converting Provençal into French but French into Provençal. Yet it was true that during Mistral's youth the bourgeoisie prided themselves on their French and aped the manners of the capital, and that the old language had disintegrated into a number of local patois spoken by the peasantry. Thus the aim of Roumanille and Mistral was not so spurious as is often claimed, since they sought merely to restore the status quo. Poetry was but the medium, the vehicle which was to revive, purify and propagate the old language.

At this time Joseph Roumanille seems to have had little faith in the future of Provence and its language, but by degrees he caught the infectious enthusiasm of the young Mistral, as, together with another pupil of the school, Anselme Mathieu, they talked of hopes and possibilities. The moment came, however, for a brief parting of the ways as Roumanille left the school to become overseer at the printing establishment of Francois Séguin in the old Hôtel de Brancas in the Rue Bouquerie, while about the same time, in 1847, Frédéric completed his course at the school and went to Nîmes to take his Baccalauréat. It was late summer, just before Mistral's seventeenth birthday. He has recorded with what trepidation he journeyed to Nîmes with his parents' blessing and, no less valuable, 150 golden francs in his pocket, of his shyness on encountering candidates from wealthy and influential families accompanied by their haughty parents, and of the awe-inspiring yellow-gowned professors of Montpellier who examined him. But he passed. And when he entered a cafe of the people to refresh himself and shyly told the market gardeners there of his success, they danced a farandole in his honor, for it was not within their experience that a son of the soil should win academic honors.

Frédéric now spent a year at home in Maillane, helping a little with the farm work but being allowed sufficient leisure to study and to write, and in particular to seek out all he could about the life of the fields and the peasant. Before his eighteenth birthday he had written a long poem in four cantos, *Li Meissoun (The Harvests)*, describing the Provençal harvest at first hand as he helped to garner the wheat before the midsummer sun set the farmlands aglow like a brazier, the harvesters moving lithely like classical figures through the golden sea of grain. The poem recalled Virgil's *Georgics*, but it was never published in its original form.

This idyll was interrupted in February, 1848 by the startling news that there had been another revolution in Paris. Louis Philippe, put on the throne as a constitutional monarch, had assumed some of the powers of a dictator, though much was to be said in his favor, and the Utopian idealists and the howling mobs crowding about the barricades set up once again in the streets of the capital had forced the aged monarch to abdicate. The Orléans family had followed the Bourbons into exile. One may suppose that it was fashionable even then to be an angry young man, and one may suppose further and hold that a young man had not his heart in the right place if he did not rebel against the accepted order of things. Young Mistral then had his heart in the right place for he became an enthusiastic supporter of the revolutionaries and the new Republic. A spirit of fierce partisanship split the entire country. Even in Maillane the community was divided into two bitterly opposed factions, the Reds and the Whites. The Reds wore red ties and sashes, the Whites wore green; the Reds carried bouquets of thyme, the Whites royalist fleurs-de-lys; the Reds planted "trees of liberty," and the Whites cut them down at night, when fights ensued and knife blades gleamed in the moonlight. Frédéric himself danced the *Carmagnole* with other rebellious youths while they sang the famous war cry of the radicals:

> *Plantons le thym, plantons le thym,*
> *Républicains, il reprendra!*
> *Faisons, faisons la farandole*
> *Et la montagne fleurira.*

He even wrote a poem waging eternal war on kings which was published in several newspapers of the region. This was too much for Mistral *père*, who for once chided his son and remonstrated with him. "But what have they done to you, these poor kings?" the old man asked, and then he delved into his own youth and told Frédéric a thing or two about the nature of revolution and revolutionaries.

Meanwhile Joseph Roumanille fought the good fight with all the resources he could muster, contributing articles, stories and ballads to the Press, good Royalist and Catholic that he was. A well known Republican encountering him in the street at this time saluted him thus: "We are of the same stock; give me your hand, brother Roumanille, that hand which makes the sign of the cross."

The forlorn hopes of the February barricades, the visions of universal suffrage, vanished with the insurrection of the starving unemployed that had followed the suppression of the shortlived national workshops in Paris. The people had had enough bickering. The cry now was for law and order. A National Assembly replaced the provisional government that had been set up, and Louis Napoleon came out of exile to become Deputy and then President of the Constituent Assembly. Mistral and Roumanille could lay down their swords and reunite for the Cause, the only Cause that really mattered—Provence.

Before the year was out it was decided to send Frédéric, after the *vendanges*, to read law at the University of Aix-en-Provence, where he duly arrived to take up studies in the Faculty of Law lodged in the Palace of the University, which was founded in 1409 and lay within the precincts of the medieval cathedral of Saint Sauveur. The old capital of Provence had not yet been shorn of many of the symbols of its past greatness, the University had not yet transferred its faculty of medicine to Marseilles (though the Law and Arts schools remain in Aix). The undergraduates were to be recognized by the *faluche* or velvet bonnet decorated with the arms of the city of Aix.

Aix was, and continues to be, one of the most beautiful of all French towns, classical in its grey tones and adagio moods, with its ubiquitous fountains adorning every little square and its Cours Mirabeau in which plane trees made a vault of greenery like an *allée couverte*. In the Cours one fountain was dominated by the figure of Good King René, another, ossified and quite Baroque, distilled tepid water, and in yet another fey children rode on swans to an entr'acte of water music. On one side of the Cours flowed the patrician houses of the *grand siècle*, turned to ivory and dull gold by the sun. This side, following tradition, belonged to the Right, while the other side belonged to the Left. People discriminated and deliberately chose which side they would be seen on, according to the color of their blood or their politics. Mistral, his political fever not yet abated, no doubt chose the Left, particularly since this side of the Cours held the bookshops and the cafes, notably the Café Sauvaire (where later Maurice Barrès wrote *Printemps à Mirabeau*) and the then quite new Café des deux Garçons with its Empire decorations. Aix was not yet preeminently the town of Cézanne and Emile Zola.

Little has been recorded of the period in Aix. Letters from Mistral to his friend of Avignon schooldays, Anselme Mathieu, make it clear that he was still in a rebellious frame of mind, trying to convert Mathieu to socialism. So that, for the time being at any rate, the lives of Mistral and Roumanille continued to run counter, for the latter was busy speaking for Christianity and Democracy for such bodies as the Societé de la foi (on which the Society of Saint Vincent de Paul was to be modelled) and in newspapers like the Avignon *Commune*, which was the first paper to sell for one copper. Letters to Mathieu also suggest that Mistral was bored, even horrified, by Sundays in Aix. Certainly he spent most weekends jaunting with friends about the countryside, to the Tholonet, to the Valley of the Inferno, where the students duelled with pistols charged with goats' droppings, to the Crau and the Camargue, to tipple at Trinquetaille on the edge of Arles and to sport with the girls, for Mathieu, who had now joined him in Aix, was of an amorous nature. Not for nothing did Mathieu become known as the "Félibre of Kisses," and in Aix he occupied himself with a pretty young laundress and then a baroness.

This pattern of Mistral's supposed sabbatical ennui is not as clear as it might be. It was not long ago, during the first year of his Avignon schooldays, that he had received his first communion in the Avignon church of Saint Didier, and his own memoirs refer to visits to the cathedral of Aix while he was at the University. In a letter to Paul Mariéton, written over half a century later, he recalls these student days and refers to the beautiful girls he and his comrades hoped to see at Mass or Vespers, *at* the services, *à la messe ou aux vêpres*, and not coming away from them, which would be *à la sortie de.*

During this period there was also the mysterious affair with the girl from a *mas* near his own home, whom he called Louise, with her face "recalling the Roman medals found at Saint Rémy" and her large, languorous dark eyes. He first met her at the Mas dóu Juge just before he went to Aix, but their correspondence

27

continued throughout his three years at the University. Louise made him several declarations of love. In her last letter she wrote, "I have loved but once, and I shall die with the name Frédéric engraved on my heart." They were both young, too young perhaps, and she knew that she was going to die. She took the veil of a nun and died a few years later. This vague relationship seems fraught with frustration and is the more pathetic since Mistral, even if he returned the same measure of love, was apparently powerless to do anything.

Meanwhile he was experimenting with verse. In February, 1850 he completed *Amarun*, a poem of fifty verses with qualities of realism worthy of Baudelaire, and in the following year an elegy which was equally pagan in spirit. That was the year 1851, in which he took his degree in law and returned home. What he would do with his qualifications was still a matter for conjecture, and if his parents hoped that he would enter one of the liberal professions they were by no means certain that he would do so. It is to the credit of Mistral *père* that he did not press his son to a decision. "Well, my boy," he would say, "I've done all I can for you, now it's up to you."

The group of friends interested in furthering the cause of Provençal letters now frequently met in Avignon, where, wrote Aubanel, "at night the stars come to dance." They gathered in one of those solid patrician houses which today are a little fly-blown in the Rue de la Banisterie, the narrow twisting cobbled street behind the Palais des Papes that runs to the chapel of the Pénitents Noirs—mildly rococo, on its façade a Gloria encircling the head of John the Baptist on a platter borne by angels, and within, like a miniature ballroom, a wealth of crystal and richly carved and gilded woodwork, medallions and ceiling.

The group consisted originally of Mistral, Roumanille, Aubanel, Mathieu and Giéra. Théodore Aubanel, whose father was official printer to the Holy See in Avignon, was after Mistral the most significant of all the Félibrige poets and it has been said that he was to Mistral what Catullus was to Virgil. Of solid bourgeois stock, he normally spoke French, was highly sensitive, was a fervent member of the confraternity of Pénitents Blancs, and collected pictures and *objets d'art*. His later life, as we shall see, was overshadowed by several unhappy events, and it must have been obvious from the beginning that there would be a clash with Roumanille, to whom he was opposed by temperament. Mathieu, whom we have already met, was the son of a prosperous peasant in Châteauneuf-du-Pape, and he endeared himself to Mistral by his eccentricities and his braggadocio concerning supposed love affairs. Paul Giéra was a notary given to banter and joking—'O *fin railleur*,' cried Mistral of him—who lived at the Château Font-Ségugne three leagues out of Avignon along the Vaucluse road.

They were all firm friends and frequently visited each other's homes. They would go to Aubanel's house, once the spired palace of a cardinal, in the Rue Saint-Marc, where in the entrance hall one could not but notice the wooden printing press on which for some two hundred years the religious literature of the various parishes and the works of the scholars of the Comtat had been printed. The visitors were a little intimidated by the church-like atmosphere and odor which seemed to have remained in the very walls of the house, but they were more awed by the old cook Jeanneton, who would grumble and mutter "Here they are again —more work." They were soon put at their ease, however, by Aubanel's father and by his uncle, who was a canon of the cathedral. The old priest was a good story-teller. One night, he said, he was called to give Extreme Unction to one of the unfortunate women of the brothels near the Madeleine. After administering to the dying woman he returned with his sacristan down the stairs, to find the staircase lined with the women of the house,

29

either half-naked or garish with the glitter and frippery of carnival. They all saluted him, their heads inclined a little to one side, with such an air of contrition that one might have supposed they had all been given absolution. The harpy in charge of the establishment meanwhile accompanied him all the way, inventing pretexts to excuse her way of life. But the old priest continued tight-lipped down the stairs, and not until the front door was opened for him did he go back and give the harpy a piece of his mind.

They would go to Roumanille's home in Saint Rémy, the simple Mas des Pommiers or House of the apple trees, with its canopy of vines. This was the house in which Joseph Roumanille was born, and his parents and his sisters Zine and Antoinette, both sparkling-eyed brunettes in their twenties, would welcome them and prepare a meal. The old market gardener Roumanille *père*, like Mistral's father, had served with the Grand Army and, so he said, had won the Cross of the Legion of Honor at Waterloo but had not bothered to claim it after the defeat.

Then they would go to Giéra's home at Font-Ségugne, strictly a *castelet* and not a château, a house resembling a large Early Victorian English villa on an estate which before the Revolution had belonged to the Dukes of Gadagne. Later, for some mysterious reason, it was bequeathed with a considerable fortune to an Avignon grocer, Baptiste Giéra, from which it passed to his elder son, Paul. It was a pleasant house and the Giéras were comfortably off, and as the future birthplace and home of the Félibrige its trees and groves and fountains were sung by the poets. Both Paul and his brother Jules were handsome, and an oil painting of the latter by Joseph Aubanel (brother of Théodore) gives Jules the dark satanic look of a Bonaparte. But Jules, though interested in poetry, was more occupied with philosophy and theology and with the work of the Pénitents Blancs. Then there were the mother, Madame Giéra, and her two daughters, Clarisse and Josephine.

Into this serene life suddenly burst the bombshell of the coup d'état of December 1, when Louis Napoleon overthrew the Constitution and, on the following day, the proclamation of the Second Empire with Louis as Napoleon III. Mistral with his fears of further centralization was indignant and perturbed. He saw this as another threat to his beloved Provence, which only a little over half a century ago had lost its rights and autonomy to a regime centralized in Paris. Now the people were threatened with further measures of regimentation, with commercial exploitation, and, worst of all, with standardized education and the probable loss of their own tongue.

Standing on the threshold of the Mas dóu Juge in Maillane, Mistral was conscious of all that was at stake. He would look around him and scan the horizon. There beyond Saint Rémy with its monuments of Roman Glanum rose the lilac-tinted Alpilles, where, held fast by the fangs of limestone, lay the incredible ruined and petrified village of Les Baux, and about it surged the stony sea of the Crau, with its nomadic shepherds, falling to the salty lagoons of the Camargue, with its cattlemen and wild horses. And there, on the Mediteraneon shore, stood the shrine of the Holy Maries. Nearer home there was Arles, the Arles of Saint Trophîme, where early Christian and Roman tradition met in the Alyscamps, the Arles of the beautiful Arlésiennes, while near it lay the Benedictine Abbey of Montmajour, burial place of the ancient Kings of Arles and Counts of Provence. On the other side of Maillane there was the abbey of Frigolet. Beyond that lay Avignon of the Popes and the indomitable Saint Catherine of Siena. Opposite, the fortress of Villeneuve was piled high above the Rhône, and upriver stood Beaucaire with its great annual fair rivalling that of Nijni-Novgorod in the Russian *steppes*, while on the *Royaume* bank was its twin Tarascon and the castle of King René, home of Saint Martha and the fabulous Tarasque. And as

31

outsiders to all this there was Orange and Nîmes, with their Roman contributions to the splendor of the classical world—not so far from Mont Ventoux, where Petrarch meditated on the nature of life and death—and ancient stranded seaports like the walled *bastide* of Aigues-Mortes. All this was "Rhodanie," that part of Provence which he loved and knew intimately.

Open to foreign influences and new ideas both by the Mediterranean and the Rhône, it was a unique product of the clash of cultures, and the terrain was made homogeneous only by the universal culture of the olive, that ancient crown of Provence, by the language and life of the people, and by the memories of the great classical civilization which had been outshone by the light of the Cross. This homogeneity was particularly marked in the farming communities, for the life of one *mas* was much the same as another—the olive harvest, the corn harvest, the *vendange*, the home production of silk, when the girls gathered the mulberry leaves for the silkworms and wound the threads of the cocoons, and the *transhumance* or spring migration of the sheep, when the shepherds led their charges to the cooler mountain pastures of Dauphiné and the Basses-Alpes, not to return until the first cool breath of autumn. Down in the Camargue the life was even more Theocritean, for there the *gardians* or cattlemen wrestled with the horns of wild bulls, as the Greeks did in Thessaly, and the peasants who lived an almost amphibious life still held the *martegado* or right to catch the fish that were benumbed by the ice, as they held the *segado* or right to cut reeds in the marshes for making mats and baskets.

It was now but a few weeks to Christmas. Already the celebrations in preparation for the Epiphany had begun, for early in December it was the custom to place grains of corn in a dish of water, the soaked grains soon bursting into minute threads. If by Christmas these tiny shoots had grown tall and strong enough, then the New Year would be filled with blessings. This "Sainte Barbe corn" was then used to adorn the table and the *crèche* or crib, itself filled with *santons* or 'holy ones,' the gaily-painted little baked-clay statues of Provence still made by about a score of families between Marseilles and Avignon. These delightful figures ranged from the little Jesus in his manger, attended by the Virgin, Saint Joseph and the Magi, to the local representative types—the flour-speckled miller, the onion-seller, the flower-girl, the drummer, the wood-cutter, moonfaced country women in the round *couqueto* coiffe of Marseilles, farandole dancers in Arlésian costume, a gypsy and his caravan.

Calèndo (Christmas) came at last. With what nostalgia did Mistral write of it in those passages ultimately omitted from *Mirèio:*
Ah! Calèndo, Calèndo, ounte èi ta douco pas? . . . Ah! Christmas, Christmas, where is thy gentle peace? Where are the smiling faces, the little children and the young girls? Where is the calloused and trembling hand of the old man who made the sign of the cross over the sacred meal?

On Christmas Eve the laborers went home early, and Madame Mistral gave each one a cake, a piece of nougat, a handful of dried figs, a cheese, a celery and a bottle of wine. Then the family and the house servant went out in search of the Yule log, which traditionally should be a branch of an olive tree or some other fruit tree (excepting a fig) which had died in the past year. On returning to the *mas* they filed three times round the kitchen, after which Mistral *père* recited a verse giving thanks to God as his "calloused and trembling hand" placed the log on the fire and then poured wine over it. As this *bûche de Nöel* burned all cried *"Cacho-fiò arrive. Tout bien arrive!"* This ceremony was the 'Tréfois' or *Cacho-fiò*, and it corresponded to the fire of Saint Jean in summer, preserving, despite the above incantation, its religious significance.

33

Then the family gathered for the traditional Christmas Eve dinner known as the *gros souper*, usually taken in front of the *crèche*. The room itself was decorated with fruit and flowers. The table was ritually covered with three cloths and dressed for the three feasts of Christmas, the Circumcision and Epiphany, and lighted with three candles in memory of the Holy Trinity, while at each corner was a plate containing some of the "Saint Barbe corn" (which also had a pagan significance since it was the symbol of the resurrection of Osiris, the grain god).

The meal was *maigré*, without meat. First snails, then fried cod and mullet, usually served with sauce *en raïto*—eaten on the eve of Christmas just as it was eaten by the Greeks on the eve of winter—or with the garlic-perfumed mayonnaise called *l'Aiòli*. Then cardoon and blanched celery. Sometimes eels were served *en raïto*. Then followed the traditional *les treize desserts*, the thirteen sweets, which was an essential feature of the dinner and recalled Christ and his twelve Apostles at the Last Supper. These were usually (though they varied from one region to another) dried grapes, small cakes in oil, almonds, raisins, nougat, fennel-scented milk cakes, apples and pears, crystallized fruits, jam or jelly, a local soft white cheese and a special Christmas cake, served with wine and liqueurs, especially the *vin cuit* of the region. Finally there was the enormous loaf of bread which could not be eaten until a quarter of it had been given to a beggar.

"The evening, waiting for midnight Mass, was long on that day; and round the fire there was lengthy talk of ancestors and praise of their actions. But little by little, and willingly, my good father would return to Spain and to his memories of the siege of Figueras."

Then came the moment to walk out into the darkness to the church, the entire family in the traditional Provençal costume which was then habitually worn. The men wore flat-brimmed felt

hats, very short jackets, and moleskin trousers with a red sashlike
flannel belt. And the women were sumptuous in the splendid regalia of Arles—the *enveloppe* or *manteau* with floral figuring of
varying patterns and colors, the *jupe* or skirt, the tight-fitting *eso*
or bodice, of which the front was called the *chapelle* because all
the jewels were on show there, the *foulard* or goffered lace collar
and the brilliant *fichu*, all built up like an architectural monument,
the sculptured head surmounted with the crowning pinnacle, the
ruban or little Phrygian bonnet of black velvet and muslin.

In the little steepled church chubby angels with gold-trimmed
wings were already standing in the choir. Then as one of them
announced the glad tidings of the birth of the Saviour a solemn
procession of shepherds in great Franciscan cloaks, with their
shepherdesses in shawls and head-dresses and carrying gifts, entered the church. At their head, following the old shepherd-in-
chief, there came a ram drawing *la caretuno*, the little intricately-
carved and candle-starred chariot in which lay a beribboned new-
born lamb on a pallet of golden straw. In their wake came the
galoubet and *tambour* players, the pipers and drummers. Before
the altar steps the old shepherd handed the lamb to his shepherd-
ess, and she in turn passed it to the next retainer, until one by one
all passed down the aisle to make their obeisance to the Agnus
Dei. Thus did the Adoration of the Shepherds become reality.

This rite of *pastrage* is still carried out at Christmas in a number of churches in Provence, notably at Les Baux—where the shepherdesses wear the *garbalin* or conical hat adorned with lace and
fruits, and the children have upon their heads the golden star of
Bethlehem, for Balthazar himself is said to have founded the little
town—at Saint Cézaire in Arles, Luceram, Frigolet, Peille, Fours
and Allauch, where the shepherds stay up all night by candlelight.
Offerings of the soil and of the sea were also made at this midnight
Mass, both as religious rites and as earnests of prosperity in the

coming year. Thus in Marseilles fishermen offered fish, and at Signes lemons (for Saint Eloi) were offered. In the Maillane *pastorale* dialogue took place between the peasants, gypsies and thieves on one side, and Our Lady and the angels on the other, but whereas Our Lady and the angels spoke in French the peasants spoke in Provençal. (Mistral was to alter this and to prevail upon the clergy to allow Our Lady and the angels to speak in Provençal also.)

All these things must have confirmed Mistral's resolve to save his country, to save all the happy, unsophisticated world of his youth and childhood, or what was left of it, and there was then a good deal. It may well have been that Christmas following so closely upon the proclamation of the Second Empire that finally brought the compelling vision of his mission. Within a few months—it was now 1852—"one evening, at seed time, when the ploughs were at work," he began *Mirèio*.

CHAPTER 3

The Seven Gay Félibres

IT WAS IN 1852 that the first anthology of contemporary poets of the *langue d'oc*, collected by Joseph Roumanille, was published in Avignon, revealing Mistral, Aubanel, Mathieu and Roumanille himself as poets to be reckoned with, while the preface by Saint-René Taillandier, the critic, referred to Mistral as "the counsellor, the censor, the severe but sympathetic judge" of the movement. For the moment, however, Roumanille was still the business brain of the group and the would-be reformer of the dialects of the Midi, and on August 29 he organized the first congress of poets in a room of the old Archbishop's Palace in Arles. The main purpose of these congresses was to bring together all the writers of the *langue d'oc* in an attempt to solve their linguistic differences and arrive at a common standard of grammar and spelling acceptable to all, for the few meridional poets who continued to use the language had largely accepted the French orthography and had added further anomalies of their own.

The choice of Arles for this first meeting was an appropriate one, for while it was to become with Avignon a focal point of the entire Félibrean movement Mistral had a regard for it far above Avignon or indeed any other place in Provence short of his own Maillane. Was it not the home of the beautiful Arlésiennes, and did it not become the home of his Museon Arlaten and the center of his *Fèsto Vierginenco*? Here the Romans had brought their brilliance along the Via Aurelia which running from Rome to Cadiz passed through the city, thus bringing also something of Spain. The Roman arena, as frankly hideous as Nero, had then only recently been cleared of the houses built within it, and like the nearby antique theatre it stood derelict and crumbling. But the sun-baked golden façade of Saint Trophime threw its living, long cool shadow across the Place de la République, the carved medieval figures of its front and cloister hieratic and almost eastern in their rich imagery. On this square with its Egyptian obelisk stood the Hôtel de Ville, a dignified Corinthian mass in which one of the celebrated Mansart brothers had a hand, with a Renaissance belfry crowned with a bronze figure of Mars, *l'homme de bronze*. Beyond it lay the Place des Hommes (now the Place du Forum), filled with bistros, where men were hired at the annual fair, and where some columns of the Roman forum were embodied in the hotel which had sheltered Merimée and Stendhal.

On the Boulevard des Lices stood the former chapel of the Carmelite nuns who, with the Archbishop of Arles, were massacred in the Revolution, and beside it was all that was left of the convent (today converted into a hotel). The façade of the chapel has a relief of cherubs sailing on clouds, and the internal rococo frothiness repeats this motif in sculptured medallions, while the high altar is surmounted with a large relief of a horse-drawn chariot riding the clouds against the gilded and starlike rays of the sun. It was the Carmelites of Arles who introduced the local vogue for the *crèche* mounted with *santons*, and for the *beatiho* or little gabled shrines made by the nuns, that were to be found in the people's homes.

Beyond, on the edge of the town, lay the Alyscamps, a surviving fragment of the celebrated Greco-Roman burial ground sung by Dante and Ariosto, its *allée des tombeaux* flanked by ancient tombs and sarcophagi which swarm with microscopic red insects. It had such a reputation in the Middle Ages that, so legend has it, bodies were floated down the Rhône in wooden coffins containing enough money to pay for their burial there. Then, the Alyscamps had no less than seventeen churches and chapels, and in Mistral's time a number remained, but they have almost all gone, and the groves of cypresses have been hacked down and the sacred precinct so abandoned that even the birds venture with timidity. The Rhône on its way to the sea flowed alongside the medieval ramparts, and a heaving bridge of boats on which the local youth danced then crossed the river to Trinquetaille, beyond which lay the Camargue. A huddle of narrow streets ended abruptly at the river, and here the scent of the apple orchards about the town mingled with the stench of open drains. Here too there were hidden churches, some now abandoned, like that of Saint Martin, which had a small dome and a balcony from which one almost expected a muezzin to call the people to prayer. About it at one time were gathered the Jews of the town.

There was perhaps something slightly Semitic in the women of Arles, in their fine proud features and golden pallor blooming with the dark blood of Greeks and Romans, Arabs and Celts. *Les Arlésiennes!* How straight and serene, graceful and dignified they looked in their traditional dress, the ebony hair built up into the local coif and sweeping above the ears, the lobes of which were studded perhaps with gilt earrings, whether in the morning with their coiffure *à l'anceu* or in the afternoon in their full regalia, *en grande tenue*. And in the evening these young belles would make the promenade along the Boulevard des Lices, like the *paseo* of Spain.

The Arles meeting did not achieve its primary purpose, and it was snubbed by Jasmin, who would have nothing to do with it, though Victor Gélu turned up. Nor did another in the following year, held in the Hôtel de Ville of Aix and attended by Emile Zola, then a boy of sixteen, when Mistral read the first of his major short poems *La Fin dóu Meissounié* (*The Death of the Harvester*), which may have derived from his earlier poem and which must be noticed at a later date when it was published in *Lis Isclo d'Or*. An indirect product of these meetings was a second slim volume of verse edited by Roumanille. In gratitude for Maillane having been spared the cholera in 1854, Mistral wrote a canticle to Our Lady of Grace. Before that, however, the year was marked by a greater and more significant event—the foundation of the Félibrige.

It was on Sunday, May 21, "in the full spring of life and of the year," that seven poets met at the Château de Font-Ségugne. They were Mistral, Roumanille, Aubanel, Mathieu, Giéra, Tavan and Brunet. The addition of the last two made the number reach the mystic seven. Alphonse Tavan was a peasant laborer from Châteauneuf-du-Gadagne who, according to Mistral, sang simply and sadly of life but who, bending over his hoe, would also sing to the sun like the cricket on the ground; at the Aix meeting he had scored a success with his poem *Li Frisoun de Marieto* or *Mariette's Curls*. Jean Brunet hailed from Avignon and appears to have been a kind of odd-job man, making a precarious living as painter and glazier, fireman and antique dealer; he often wore a painter's smock, and he had, wrote Mistral, "the face of Christ of Galilee."

The actual launching of the Félibrige was something of a semireligious act, for it was immediately preceded by Mass where all took communion, though Brunet seems to have kicked against it before following suit. It was the feast day of Saint Estelle, who was adopted as the patron saint of the new society, while the seven-pointed star of the saint became the society's emblem. But who was this Saint Estelle or Estello who even today appears under May 21 in the annually published calendar of the *Armana*

Prouvençau? Was she not invented by the Félibrige, a creation of Mistral's mind, or perhaps a symbol invented by Paul Giéra, the astrologer and philosopher? Yet it is strange, to say the least of it, to see this Saint Estelle raised to the throne of God, for in Mistral's written testament on the inauguration of the Félibrige is the following:

> *Au nom du Père et du Fils et du Saint Esprit,*
> *et de Sainte Estelle, patron du Félibrige,*
> *ainsi soit-il—moi, Frédéric Mistral, poète,*
> *provençal de Maillane en Provence, soussignè.*

At this more than usually important feast, then, they adopted a seven-pointed emblem. There were seven of them, they drank a Châteauneuf-du-Pape which had been seven years in bottle, and it was probably no mere coincidence that seven was a denominator in the date. Strangely, there are seven letters in each of the words 'Mistral' and 'Félibre,' and Mistral apparently spent seven years in writing each of his epic poems. The poets liked to say of Avignon that seven popes resided there over seventy years, and that the city had seventeen churches, seven gates, seven colleges and seven hospitals. Certainly Mistral's half-serious, half-laughing regard for the predictions of Nostradamus colored many of his activities, and it seemed that not even his faith could entirely shake a conviction that the world was governed by mysterious and even mystic laws.

Mistral himself baptized the new society. "My friends," he said, "there is an old folk-song which contains our chosen word where it is said that the Virgin found Jesus in the temple among *les sept félibres de la loi.*" The reference was to the traditional theme of the Seven Sorrows of Our Lady, and more particularly to the young Jesus disputing with the Doctors or *félibres* of the Law. The origin and meaning of the word led to much argument.

Nobody quite knew what it meant, and philologists wrangled over it and paraded their learning. Mistral himself frankly confessed to inquisitive visitors that it had no particular meaning. Six years later he wrote to his friend William Bonaparte-Wyse asking him to trace the origin of the Irish word *filea*, which Mistral thought might have some bearing on the derivation of *félibre*. The poet went on to remark that O'Reilly's Irish Dictionary contained the word *feliber*, compounded of *feli* or poet and *par* (identical with *ber* or king). In the same letter he mentions other derivations put forward by various philologists—the Latin *felibris,* a disciple; the Greek *philebraios* or lover of the beautiful; the Hebrew *sephem* (*de la Lèi*); and the Spanish *feligres* meaning a parishioner or follower. Quite obviously it was a subject for the most exciting speculation, and nobody could say that the Félibrige was specifically this or specifically that—a great advantage. It was in fact a brilliant stroke on Mistral's part, one of those strokes of genius which enabled his disparagers to accuse him of showmanship.

Félibres of the Law? What law? asked one of the seven at this historic meeting. Mistral then promised that he would compile the 'Law' of the Félibres. The statutes, the organization in a strict hierarchy with a central consistory did not come until later. For the moment it was enough that they had banded together to restore the old language, to stimulate the local patriotism of the Provençaux, to retain the old customs and promote the study of local history, to encourage the regional music and the arts of the people, in short to manifest to the world that this ancient *Provincia* had a soul and a distinct individuality of its own. It was not a back-with-the-clock movement nor was there anything archaic about it; it was simply the defense and maintenance of living values. As Bonaparte-Wyse, in an address at Forcalquier some years later, put it in his customary honeyed phrases, "Félibrige means the cult of the good, of the beautiful, of the true, through

42

the medium of the sweet mother-tongue." What Mistral meant by the 'Law' at this juncture, however, was nothing less than his Provençal encyclopaedia-dictionary, *Lou Tresor dóu Felibrige*, though the compilation of this enormous work was to take over three decades. It was also decided to publish annually the *Armana Prouvençau* or Provençal Almanac, which had nothing in common with popular almanacs like that of Old Moore (though, true to Nostradamus, Mistral did write in it an essay on popular astronomy).

Looking at photographs of the new troubadours as they were grouped on the steps of Font-Ségugne on that historic day, the unsympathetic may perhaps detect traces of smug exuberance and self-satisfaction, something a little histrionic.

> *Nous sommes des amis, des frères . . .*
> *C'est nous qui sommes les félibres*
> *Les gais félibres provençaux.*

All excepting Tavan were mustached and bearded, and the most handsome were Paul Giéra and Mistral, who at twenty-four already had the small goatee beard which he retained all his life. The youngest was Tavan, who had just attained his majority, and the oldest was Giéra, who, born in 1816, was two years older than Roumanille. They all look solemn and dedicated rather than smug, and indeed there is little to suggest "the gay Félibres" and the Empire of the Sun. There is, however, ample evidence of their *joie de vivre* and capacity for fun, and of their humanity, in their wine-flowing feasts, their far-ranging excursions and literary picnics, which in the early days often resembled the pranks and escapades of schoolboys. They wandered at midnight in the Alyscamps of Arles, under the stars and *le Chemin de Saint Jacques* (*la voie lactée* or the Milky Way), chanting among the silent tombs. They sang robust songs to flatter and embarrass the lovely Arlésiennes.

43

They dined on Gargantuan helpings of *l'aioli* and *bouillabaisse* in homely taverns, and they scandalized the innkeeper by their hilarious banter, as they delighted the peasants with their verses. They set out for Mont Ventoux and were arrested as vagabonds. They looked for eagles and the *Chèvre d'Or* in the Alpilles, and on the stony roads of the Crau Aubanel would chant his *Vénus d'Arles*. They would flock into the Avignon restaurants of the day —the Auberge Saint Omer, the Hôtel de la Mule, the Chêne-Vert and the old waterside inn near the reeds of the Ile de Barthelasse. From this island in the Rhône, facing the ramparts of the city, they would climb up to Villeneuve, where from the fortified hilltop they would look across to Avignon's rock-bound Papal Palace floating, apparently, on a soft bed of waving green foliage shot with seams of silver and russet, and, islanding the city, the fields of corn and teazle and lucerne, the vines and mulberry trees and the black-pointed cypresses, all fading away to the heights of the Alpilles. Or they would go on to Châteauneuf-du-Pape, the home of Mathieu and of the glorious wine which Daudet dubbed "royal, imperial and pontifical," with its annual procession in honor of Saint Peter of Luxembourg and its vintners' fête in honor of Saint Mark.

They were often accompanied by their wives and *chatos* or sweethearts, the *damisello graciouso* or pretty girls who were often to be seen at Font-Ségugne. There was always a bevy of such girls at the Château, among them Mistral's cousins Gango, Villette and Lali, Roumanille's sisters Zine and Antoinette, the Giéra girls Clarisse and Josephine, and others like Julia and Jenny Manivet. With their gallants they would stroll among the groves of oaks, planes and acacias, and they would sing or recite verses, to be answered by the song of the crickets, the nightingales and the tree frogs. It was here that Aubanel fell under the spell of Jenny Manivet, the Zani of the poets. Later he was to sing her praises in his *Book of Love*, of "her slender figure and her woollen dress—the color of the pomegranate—her brow so smooth and her large eyes so beautiful, her long black hair and her dusky face . . ." He even wrote verses on the walls of the room where she had lain at the Château: "When I pass by your threshold, oh little room, I say to myself *They are coming*—I imagine that I see you, oh, beautiful maidens—thou poor Julia, thou, my dear Zani—but no longer will you sleep in the little room—Julia, thou art dead! Zani, thou art a nun!"

It was true. Jenny had abandoned her lover, family and Félibrige and, like Louise, had taken the veil. It is said that her Order of Saint Vincent de Paul sent her to the East, where she died in the same year as Aubanel without ever having seen him again. Another source suggests, however, that she returned to Provence just after Aubanel's death and herself died in the following year. Whichever way it was, the renunciation was complete and final, and Aubanel wrote of his passion and grief in his *Mióugrano entreduberto* (*The Cleft Pomegranate*), which like a later book of his received the censure of the Church and was placed on the *Index*. But was his Zani really so beautiful? Photographs show her to be a darkly complexioned young woman, slightly negroid, with hard thin lips and the stamp of asceticism.

And what of Mistral in this galaxy of youth and beauty. Did he have no affairs of the heart, was there not perhaps another Louise? Or was he remaining true to his mother and holding fast to his Rhodanie and the Cause?

It was on May 24 of the following year that Mistral and Mathieu made the pilgrimage from Beaucaire to Les Saintes. There were forty pilgrims in the overcrowded cart in which the two friends made the journey, and the other wagons in the cavalcade were equally overcrowded. Among their companions was a pretty girl who, abandoned by her lover, was crying and murmuring to herself. The caravan was overtaken by a storm, and it was necessary for the party to descend and trudge for several kilometres along a road deluged with rain and mud, whereupon the gallant Frédéric carried the beautiful young innocent upon his shoulders. A French critic has seen in this incident a full measure of symbolism. Did not Mistral (he suggests) carry *la belle Provence* upon his shoulders, did he not raise his miserable native language out of the mire?

The wagoner driving Mistral's party was a hefty *roulier de Provence* named Lamouroux, who told the poet something of the company of the roads before the coming of the railway—"*Ah! messieurs, je vous parle de l'époque du roulage.*" He described the inns on the roads between Marseilles and Avignon and Paris, and the dress of the wagoners with their blue shirts, velvet breeches and gaiters, their colored bonnets and great woollen capes bellying out behind them in the wind. Sometimes they sang as they marched along beside their horses, one hand on the bridle rein and in the other a whip, and they shouted greetings in Provençal to other wagoners who passed by. Sometimes the wagoners fought with whips and stones until one of them died. From Marseilles to Lyons they walked on the left of their horses, but at Lyons this Provençal custom ceased and they changed to the right. Northwards came the heavy rains which turned the roads into quagmires. But the joys of Paris then lay ahead, and the wagoners would enter the capital to the sound of cracking whips. Lamouroux declared gaily that the Parisians would put their hands to their ears as they heard the whips in the distance, crying out "*Allons! les Provençaux arrivent!*"

And now they were in the Camargue, a moody prairie-like country choked with sand and tufts of spiky grasses, with salt marsh and brown-green blotches of samphire and gillyflower. At intervals there was a cluster of thatched cabins surrounded by tamarisk trees, or an occasional *mas* islanded in a patch of vineyard and grazing land. There were gleaming threads of silver on the horizon, and soon they were passing by the edge of the Vaccarès lagoon. On this day all roads led to Les Saintes, and the way was now heavy with an odd collection of horsedrawn vehicles, the *voitures, roulottes* and *guimbardes* and the caravans of the gypsies on the way to the shrine of black Sara. The gaunt fortress tower which for so long had dominated the vast empty sky merged into sharper detail, and the embattled church of large larva blocks was seen to be almost as window-less as the anti-Saracen fortress it virtually had been. Les Saintes Maries—known for centuries as Notre Dame de la Mer—was swarming with people. It was and remains a little town, no larger than a village, of low flat-roofed buildings, whitened or color-washed, some with wooden verandahs recalling the ranches of Arizona or the haciendas of the American south, which flowed right down to the edge of the stony beaches and the curling sea.

On the façade of Saint Trophîme in Arles is a carving of *les Saintes-Maries*—Mary Magdalen, Mary Jacobé, sister of the Virgin, and Mary Salomé, the mother of James and John. Why are they there, and why do they figure so prominently in the religious art of the Midi and the Mediterranean? In the persecution that followed the Crucifixion the family of Bethany was sent by the Jews into exile and to possible death, for they were placed on a ship without sails, oars or rudder, and the vessel was cast off to drift upon the seas. With Mary Jacobé and Mary Salomé went Lazarus and his sisters Mary Magdalen and Martha, Maximin and many others, including Sara, the Egyptian handmaiden of Saints Mary Jacobé and Mary Salomé. The winds blew the ship from the land of Judea to this desolate littoral of Provence. The saints dispersed, Mary Magdalen to the mountain cave of the Sainte-Baume, Martha to Tarascon, Lazarus to the conversion of Mar-

47

seilles and Maximin to become first bishop of Aix. Mary Jacobé, Mary Salomé and Sara remained where they landed, at what is now Les Saintes Maries de la mer. In the fifteenth century excavations directed by King René of Anjou were made beneath the church of Les Saintes Maries and what were held to be the remains of Mary Jacobé and Mary Salomé were discovered. The authenticity of the discovery largely rested on an inscribed marble slab which has disappeared with the centuries, and such prominent scholars as Charles Lenthéric and Fernand Benoit have shown that if the traditions of the Christianizing of Gaul have been disputed there is nothing to disprove them.

Mistral's party arrived, it seems, just in time for the crucial moment of the church ceremony, for the exposition of the relics, when the *chasse* or casket was lowered from its resting-place in the high belfry chapel, a Louis XV chamber of gilt and absinthe-colored panelling, by means of an elaborate system of pulley chains, garlanded for the occasion. The ceremony today is little different from what it was then, though the crowds are now denser and the gypsies have associated themselves more closely with the proceedings. The great gilded casket swings perilously in mid-air but comes finally to rest upon the high altar. The throng surges forward to kiss the reliquary. There are loud cries of *"Vivent els Saintes-Maries,"* to which the *gitans*, not to be outdone, roar *"Vive Sainte-Sara."* Though it is unlikely that Sara was raised to the altar she has inspired a rare devotion among all the Romany of Europe, and in the catacomb-like crypt she is invoked and presented with petitions even by nomads who have penetrated the Iron Curtain. Here the counterfeit likeness of the backdoor Sara is vested in a multi-colored velvet cape and decked with trinkets and a crown of wild flowers by the gypsy women, so that she resembles a sumptuous Asiatic queen.

We do not know what Mistral's emotions were on this pilgrimage or, indeed, how much of the tradition he accepted. What is certain is that *Li Santo, Les Saintes,* were inevitably and inextricably part and parcel of his Provençal upbringing and that they remained for him a compelling spiritual force until the very end of his life.

*   *   *

Joseph Roumanille had now set up a printing press, the beginning of his celebrated bookshop and printing business, in the Rue Saint Agricol, the street that leads from the Place Georges Clémenceau and passes the dark medieval church of Saint Agricol until it comes up against the airy church called the Oratoire. It was here in the year 1855 that the first copy of the *Armana Prouvençau,* capably edited by Aubanel, was printed. It has survived without a break, and though the initial circulation was only five hundred copies it reached ten thousand by the end of the century. Its brilliant cover recalls the Yellow Book of the Victorian nineties, and there was no less affinity in contents. All the writers and artists of the *langue d'oc* were to contribute to it, but the stories of Roumanille and the apologues and sketches of Mistral alone would have justified its existence. All the original seven Félibres contributed to it, and all had their pseudonyms. Thus Mistral was the Félibre of the Mas, Roumanille the Félibre of Gardens, Aubanel the Félibre of the Pomegranate, Mathieu the Félibre of Kisses, Tavan the Félibre of the Army (he was a conscript) and Brunet (who was primarily a painter) the Félibre of the Rainbow. Instructive, amusing, patriotic, it beguiled the families around Provençal hearths through the long winter nights. For the Daudet family, then 'exiled' in Lyons, its appearance provided a nostalgic link with the south. "We used to go and wait for the *Armana* when it came in," wrote Alphonse, "as men in the colonies look out for the mail boat from France."

49

Yet it was a sad year for Mistral, for September brought the death of his father. For some time the old man's sight had been failing, and the last Christmas had lacked the customary gaiety for he could no longer lead the family in the ceremony of the *Cacho-fio*; he had sat at dinner sad and silent, and all he had said was, "Last year I could still see a faint glow from the candles—now I see nothing. Help me, oh Holy Virgin." If, as he claimed, he was twenty-two when he was at the siege of Figueras, then he was born in 1772 and was now eighty-three (through Frédéric's memoirs suggest that he was two years younger). It was time to go in peace. The family gathered weeping about his bed.

"My children," said the old man, "I am going . . . and I give thanks to God for all that I owe to him, my long life and my labor, which have been blessed."

A little later he said,

"Frédéric, what is the weather doing?"

"It is raining, father."

"*Eh, bien!* if it rains it will be good weather for the sowing."

And so he died. The servants and laborers were told to stop work at once. Madame Mistral, sitting in a corner of the great chimney place, put a white fichu on her head, the traditional sign of mourning in Provence, and all day the neighbors and friends came, one after the other, with their condolences and the salute, "May Our Lord keep you."

For Frédéric this was a calamitous event, a complete break with the past. Mistral *père* indeed left such a marked impression on the mind of his son that he is immortalized in the patriarchs of Mistral's epics. His death, moreover, brought a second calamity close on the heels of the first, for the property was now divided up and the Mas dóu Juge went to the eldest son. All the familiar and loved household goods were brought out in front of the *mas* and divided by an official into three lots for the heirs. Among Frédéric's portion was a house in the village, *l'Oustau dóu Lesert*, the House of the Lizard, to which he and his mother were now slowly carried in the lumbering farm wagon which also bore those household goods allotted to them. It was autumn. The sadness must have been unbearable.

The House of the Lizard was a plain square building standing on the street, then the last house on the road to Saint Rémy. There was no front garden, but at the back there were figs and laurels, a stone well and a stone bench. Soon after moving in Mistral sculptured a lizard and three lines of verse upon a sundial over the door lintel:

> *Bèu lesert, bèu tuon soulèu,*
> *L'ouro passo que trop lèu,*
> *E, deman, ploura, belèu.*

(Beautiful lizard, drink of the sun, Time passes only too quickly and tomorrow perhaps it will rain.) This inscription, together with lines in praise of Mistral and quotations from his works, appears on the house today, but whether the niched figure of the Madonna on the angle of the building was added by Mistral is not clear. Mistral himself drank of the sun, greedily; his work was not merely the product of chambering himself with books, but of striding through the fields and walking around the village, of conversation with all the workers and of expeditions in search of living truths. This was after all the Empire of the Sun, and Lamartine, writing of Mistral and his milieu, was to say: *"Il y a une vertu dans le soleil."*

Among the first strangers to call at the House of the Lizard was Adolphe Dumas. Dumas was also a native of Provence; he was born in the ruins of an old Carthusian monastery on the banks of the Durance, and his death was to be equally improbable for he died in a fisherman's hut in Dieppe. Indeed the whole of his life seems somewhat improbable, and he might never have been given education and opportunity but for his sister. This pretty elder sister ran off with a troupe of strolling actors, but was later found, destitute and weeping, in the streets of Paris by a wealthy nobleman who, recognizing her virtues, married her. In due course she sent for young Adolphe and educated him just in time for him to be caught up in the Romantic movement of 1830. His poems and slight prose pieces are no longer read, and but for Lamartine's tribute in the *Entretiens* and the association with Mistral he might have become completely forgotten. At this time quite well known, he had been entrusted by his friend the Minister for Education with the official work of collecting the traditional folk songs of Provence, though nowhere is it indicated that he was a musician or that he had the expertise of a Cecil Sharp. In his wanderings it was but natural that he should hear of Frédéric Mistral and call upon him. Mistral seems to have taken to him at once. He found Dumas to be a man of fifty, a somewhat swashbuckling handsome dandy with ascetic pallor, long greying hair, brown mustache and little tufted beard, flaming dark eyes and a resounding voice which was almost invariably accompanied by a hand raised in the air in a dramatic gesture. He was tall but trailed a crippled leg after him, reminding Mistral of "a Provençal cypress agitated by the wind."

Mistral replied simply but effectively to Dumas' inquiry about folk songs by singing to him the song of *Magali* from *Mirèio*, on which he was then working.

> *O Magali, ma tant amado,*
> *Mete la Tèsto au fenestroun!*
> *Escouto un pau aquesto aubado*
> *De Tambourin e de Viouloun.*
> *Ei, plen d'estello, aperamount*
> *L'auro es toumbado,*

Mai li estello paliran
Quand te veiran.

(Oh Magali my beloved,
Show thy face at the window!
Hearken to this dawn song
Of violins and tambourines . . .)

This is the opening verse, and the song goes on with the girl's protestations that she will change herself into fish or hare or hunter or rose or honeybee or grass or cloud to avoid the persistent lover, and he always finding an imagined metamorphosis to win her. Finally she vows that she will even become a nun·

If thou wilt be a nun professed,
A nun of orders grey,
Then I will be the prior, and thou
To me thy sins must say,
Then will I sleep among the dead,
While the sisters weep and pray.

If thou wilt sleep among the dead,
While the sisters weep and pray,
Then I will be the holy earth
That on thee they shall lay,
If thou wilt be the holy earth
That on me they shall lay—
Well—since some gallant I must have,
I will not say thee nay.

The foregoing is not strictly a translation of Mistral's song but of the popular version which is sung from the Comtat to the Var. The theme is ancient and echoes Ovid's *Metamorphoses,* and the construction of the song may owe something to Greek Provence and an ode of Anacreon. Mistral tells us that he heard his servant singing this song, but according to M. Fernand Benoit, the historian of Provence, the tune was adapted from a ballad called *Le Retour du Rossignol (The Return of the Nightingale)*, which dated from the Napoleonic Wars. Certainly Mistral refashioned the ballad in the way that Burns refashioned the old songs of his own country. Anyway, Dumas was enthralled. "But where did you fish for this pearl?" he asked. He wanted to know more, and soon Mistral was reciting verses of his as yet unfinished *Mirèio*. It seems that Dumas was not only convinced of Mistral's genius but was also converted to the Cause on the spot, and he was to prove a staunch ally.

Shortly afterwards Mistral went with a friend, Ludovic Legré, one of the Font-Ségugne circle, to Paris. It was his first visit to the capital and he stayed a week. The Paris of that time is described in the novels of Balzac and Eugène Sue. It was still a medieval town of narrow, dim, dirty, cobbled streets lighted by oil lanterns, but the great metamorphosis had just begun. Vast areas were being cleared for the new replanned city which as yet lay only on the drawing boards of Baron Haussmann. Mistral had little time but he did see what he could from Notre Dame to the Louvre, but the Place Vendôme to the Arc de Triomphe, built only twenty years earlier. Then he called on Adolphe Dumas.

"*Eh bien*," Dumas greeted him, "This Mirèio—is she finished?"

"She is finished, and here she is—in manuscript."

On that and the following day Mistral read the entire work in three sittings to Dumas, who straightway sent a letter to the *Gazette de France* of Paris. If the letter was somewhat crude propaganda it did at least introduce to the public the man whom Dumas had deigned to call "the Virgil of Provence, the Mantuan shepherd arriving in Rome with poetry worthy of Gallus and Scipio." Nor was this the end of Dumas' services. The next day he introduced Mistral to Lamartine.

Alphonse Lamartine had by that time written almost all his

major works, from the *Méditations* of 1820 to *Le Désert* of 1856. After the revolution of 1830 he had turned to politics and advocated an idealistic Christian liberalism, gradually turning to Socialism. He had been a member of the provisional government of 1848 and a candidate for the presidency of the Republic, and his prestige and virtues had softened the ugly processes of the proletariat revolt. Under Louis Napoleon he had retired to live privately, and was now desperately turning out political histories in an effort to work off the immense debts he had accumulated during his brief tenure of office. The son of a Burgundian landowner, he had spoken until he was twelve a patois akin to Provençal, so that he had little difficulty in reading Mistral's poems. He was a man after Mistral's own heart, for he was attached to his home in the Maconnais and his family associations, and in his elegiac *Méditations* there is a poetic veneration of the places made sacred by their links with his past.

Before he left Paris Mistral called on Lamartine to say farewell. The details of these interviews are to be found in a letter from Mistral to Roumanille, from which it appears that Lamartine had already heard of Mistral, Roumanille and Aubanel from both Dumas and Jean Reboul. Mistral goes on to say that they talked about the country about Arles and the Camargue, which Lamartine knew, and that the old man then asked him to recite the opening stanzas of *Mirèio*, which he was called upon to repeat when the ladies came in. Later Lamartine was to write his own version of these meetings in his *Cours familier de Littérature*. So Mistral returned to Maillane, encouraged and perhaps justifiably pleased with himself, charged by both Lamartine and Dumas to publish *Mirèio* with all possible speed and to despatch copies to them. Strangely, nearly three years were to elapse before that event, and the fact that Mistral, painstaking as ever, polished the work even further cannot wholly account for this delay.

In the following year he wrote *L'Anounciado* (*The Annuncia-*

tion), which paraphrased the relative verses of the first chapter of Saint Luke, and *Communioun di Sant* (*Communion of Saints*), which he prepared for the feast of All Saints of that year, 1857. The latter is a mystical piece in which the poet sees the Virgin descending the steps of Saint Trophime in Arles at nightfall, and in which the saints of Arles go with the angels to assist at Midnight Mass in the Alyscamps. In the following year he wrote *l'Ase de Sant-Jóusé* (*Saint Joseph's Ass*), the canticle *Per Nosto-Damo de Roumigié* and the translation of the Magnificat. None of this was great poetry, but it was inspired by an intensity of religious emotion which later he seems to have lost for a while. This question of Mistral's faith crops up from time to time in his long life. Like Lammenais—and this seems to have been characteristic of the Romantics—Mistral's faith was sorely tested by the alliance between the Church and the régimes of the Restoration in Europe, when for him sanity lay in a *rapprochement* between the Church and the forces of liberalism. There is no evidence, however, to show that Mistral was, like Lammenais, torn between belief and unbelief, or that, like Goethe, he created a Christianity for his own personal use.

Meanwhile he must have visited the now restored abbey of Saint Martin de Frigolet, which had been purchased by Père Edmond for the Order of Prémontré, the white-habited Norbertines. The church was rebuilt, with three fine naves and two bell towers, and filled with lavish decoration. There were cells for a hundred monks and laybrothers. On Sundays in particular the people of the countryside flocked to it in their wagons to attend the impressive services, and for Mistral it must have been in some respects a droll experience as he recalled his early schooldays and poor old Monsieur Donnat, now dead. And soon Mistral saw the restoration of yet another monastery on his native terrain, for in 1859 Lacordaire's campaign to reinstate the Dominicans throughout France culminated in the opening of the monastery of Saint Maximin, with its celebrated basilica which held the mortal remains of Mary Magdalen, Maximin, Sidonia and Trophime. And if Lacordaire's hopes of reviving the popularity of *les Saints Lieux de Provence* were not entirely fulfilled, the century provided France with new saints of its own.

Mistral had by now settled in his new home, and his main activities continued to be connected with the Félibrige, with meetings and fêtes and speeches. Addressing such a gathering, largely consisting of Catalan Félibres, at Saint Rémy in 1858, he reaffirmed the Félibrean gospel as it had been formulated from the beginning:

". . . . that our children, instead of being brought up in contempt of our Provençal customs, instead of envying the baubles of Paris or Madrid, should continue to speak the language of their cradle, the gentle language of their mothers, and that they should remain in the farms where they were born, and that they should wear forever the *ruban* of Arles like a diadem; and that our people instead of wallowing in ignorance of their own history, of their great past, of their personality, should understand in short their claims to nobleness and that their fathers have the wisdom to live always as free men and to defend that right."

In November of that year he would have heard that John Stuart Mill and his wife were staying in Avignon, at the Hôtel de l'Europe, where English celebrities had stayed when making the Grand Tour, though it was not the splendid establishment that it is today and the bedrooms and sitting room were then floored with red tiles overlaid with thin worn carpet. Mill's wife died there during the month, and from then on Mill made his home in Avignon and ultimately died there. It was fitting that the man who championed the emancipation of women should adopt this terrain, for it was just above the Rhône valley that the medieval

Council of Mâcon had decreed that women possessed souls and were in fact human beings. Mistral had a healthy respect for Mill, and the highly idealized types of womanhood in his poems owe not a little to Mill's influence.

The Avignon of this time was filling with new monuments and neo-Baroque statuary at which Mistral no doubt cocked a dubious eye, for the old theatre by the Porte de l'Oulle had been abandoned for a new one, and there was a new Hôtel de Ville, both buildings being in the moribund and eclectic style which characterized the period. It was an age of pastiche. The great architect and arch-restorer Viollet-le-Duc was now at work on the rehabilitation of the Palais des Papes and the medieval ramparts, strengthening walls and adding mock fortifications and galleries, and opening new gateways, so that it all resembled the *Contes Drolatiques* of Balzac. Was it to become another Carcassonne, that inviolate walled city in Languedoc, with its galaxy of conical roofs like the steeple hats of witches? Not quite, but Viollet-le-Duc put the same concentrated effort, the same scrupulosity—or unscrupulosity—into the Avignon restoration. All the great cathedrals of France, and much else, were to pass through his hands. The result was some improvement on the erstwhile neglected and chaotic state of these monuments, but much had been lost in the process, for, significantly, the architect defined his own practice thus: "To restore a building . . . is to re-establish it in a state of completion, which may never have existed at any given moment in the past."

BOOK TWO

Symbols

Acquaint thyself with the choragium *of the Stars, and
consider the vast expansion beyond them.*

SIR THOMAS BROWNE

*I shut myself in with my soul,
And the shapes come eddying forth.*

ROSSETTI

*There is no excellent beauty that hath not some strange-
ness in the proportion.*

BACON

*. . . What might this be? A thousand fantasies
Begin to throng into my memory,
Of calling shapes, and beckning shadows dire,
And airy tongues that syllable men's names
On Sands and Shoars and desert Wildernesses . . .*

MILTON

*Tell me where is Fancy bred,
Or in the heart, or in the head?
How begot, how nourished?*

SHAKESPEARE

CHAPTER 4

Mirèio

It was on February 2, the feast of Saint Agatha, patron saint of Maillane, in 1859 that *Mirèio* (*Mireille*) was published by Roumanille in Avignon. It had taken a long time in making its appearance, and three years had passed since Mistral had taken the draft to Paris. He was a conscientious painstaking craftsman, for, as Leonardo da Vinci remarked, "He is a poor master whose work surpasses his judgement; he alone is advancing towards the perfection of art whose judgement surpasses his work." Viewed in the context of the French literary background of the period—the previous three years had seen such best sellers as Flaubert's *Madame Bovary* (1856), Baudelaire's *Les Fleurs du Mal* (1857) and Gautier's *Le Roman de la Momie* (1858)—this long poem in twelve cantos was as fresh as a spring morning.

Mirèio is a story of frustrated love in another age and another setting, and though it is embroidered with a few touches of fantasy there is little that is outside normal, or at least possible, human experience. Yet with its brilliant evocations of the South and of a life that was even then passing it has today an air of unreality, even implausibility. It is an epic, but it is a rustic epic, and it was written of the people and for the people, for Mistral knew that the essential character of Provence was closely bound up with the *gentilshommes campagnards* or yeomen farmers (our nearest equivalent to the *ménagers*), the peasant and the soil. Thus the heroine, Mirèio, is a simple country girl, even if she is the daughter of a *ménager*, and the hero, Vincèn, a poor basket maker. But within the simple framework of frustrated love—the opposition of Mirèio's parents to the match, the rival suitors who come to blows, and the tragic flight of Mirèio—there is all the life and glory of Provence; indeed it is Provence that the poet sings, and his characters are perhaps little more than symbols. What Mistral, faithful to the image of his childhood, is really lamenting is a lost innocence and a vanishing way of life. Beauty for Mistral was not an end but a way; the end was the elevation of the people.

Mèste Ambròsi and his son Vincèn, both basket makers, seek hospitality at the Mas di Falabrego, the Farm of the Mulberries, where Mirèio, daughter of Mèste Ramoun, makes them welcome. In the second canto there is a tender love scene between Mirèio and Vincèn against the background of the mulberry picking, the mulberry trees full of young girls gathering the crop of the silkworms as a flight of golden bees robs the rosemary of its sweets, and they sing with the joy of their work, *Cantas, cantas, magnanarello*. The third canto is filled with the malicious chatter and sly gossip of these *magnanarello* as they gather the cocoons of the silkworms ready for the home production of silk, and it ends with that ballad of *Magali* which so intrigued Adolphe Dumas. In the fourth canto the summer sun has fired the blood of other suitors for Mirèio's hand, to whom we are introduced one by one. The first is the shepherd Alàri, the second is Véran the *gardian* or herdsman, and the third is Ourrias the *toucadu* who rears savage bulls. Here Mistral exploits the introduction of each suitor to enlarge on an aspect of Provençal life.

Thus Alàri, a shepherd who might have stepped out of the

Scriptures, was a characteristic product of his race following the timeless and unchanging pattern of his calling. The Provençal shepherd was a semi-nomad and something of a recluse, and he spent half the year away from his master's farm and his limited circle of friends, living on remote uplands where he would probably encounter no one for months. When the heat dried up the pastures the flocks were driven from the plains and valleys into the mountains of Haute-Provence and Dauphiné and there they would remain until the first cool breath of autumn. An annual fair used to be held in Arles, late in May, heralding the departure of the flocks, and this was known as the *Foire des regrets*, since the departure of the shepherds had its element of sadness, depleting the family circles on the farmsteads. Immediately after the fair the sheep were counted, as they still are, by a numbering system of medieval origin (as Goidelic numerals are still used for counting sheep on the remote uplands of Wales). The shepherd usually had one or two assistants, and his caravan included mules, laden with equipment and provisions, and goats, which cleared difficult passages. Sometimes farmers followed their flocks, living in mountain huts as the Swiss still do and as the Welsh hill farmers formerly did, living in their *hafotai*.

The shepherd wore a kind of smock down to the middle of his thighs, breeches of coarse cloth, gaiters of skin or hide, hobnailed boots, and a bonnet-shaped hat which was probably of otter skin. In cold weather he donned a great cloak of coarse fabric with a cowllike hood. His crook or staff was probably of hazel wood, and he sometimes carried a whip of plaited thongs, while his tools and other possessions may have been carried in a scrip of leather or hide suspended from the shoulder by a large strap enriched with patterns of copper nails. His chief weapon was a large knife designed to bleed the ewes and to scrape the lambs immediately after birth.

The route he followed to the mountains was probably an old *draille* or track used by Roman shepherds. These *drailles* are still marked out for the passage of sheep, and shepherds were legally compelled to follow them, while any form of public traffic was forbidden. The tracks were of prescribed widths and varied at different periods from between ten and twenty metres to thirty metres. Some of the old routes are still used. There are, for example, two routes to Dauphiné by the Rhône Valley, one by Carpentras, and the other by the right bank following the Roman road from Saint-Gabriel via Tarascon, Beaucaire, Remoulins, Bagnols and Pont-Saint-Esprit. The route from the plain about Arles to the Passage du Verdon follows the old route from Italy into Spain. The shepherd following more remote routes found the tracks fallen into disuse, and he often spent nights in abandoned stone huts, before each of which was the original circular stone sheepfold. Sitting over his brushwood fire, scented perhaps with fennel and wild thyme, he would scan the surrounding hills for other camp fires, for migrating shepherds communicated with each other by means of such fires. He spent his days and nights alone in a lofty mountainous world, caring only for his sheep, preparing cheeses from sheep's milk, to be kept moist wrapped in fresh leaves, and perhaps carving a wooden sheep collar such as Alàri offered to Mirèio.

In October the farmers and their families eagerly look for clouds of homing sheep on the distant hills. The *retour des troupeaux* was a time of joy on the farmsteads. The folds were prepared for their return, filled with bundles of fresh straw, with hay in all the cribs, and the water troughs were cleaned out. The master would know the day of their return, and perhaps he would go into the hills to meet them. Presently he heard the barking of the dogs and the bleating of the ewes and the tinkling of copper or bronze bells (which formerly were all of different notes). And the shepherd came forward to make his report—so many new lambs and so many full ewes, the milk rich and good. It had been a long summer but he was home again.

Quite obviously, however, this would have been no life for Mirèio. Véran the *gardian* could not have given her so much more, though he belonged to a unique body of men, descendants of those trappers or cattlemen of the Fenimore Cooper type who long ago settled in the mosquito-infested marshes of the Camargue and had developed into the cowboys of France. They even had their own confraternity, founded as long ago as 1513, under the patronage of Saint George. The life that Véran lived has today lost much of its necessity and gusto and is now best seen in the paintings of Antoine Galle (1808-88) of Arles, who depicted it in a manner savoring of the *douanieri*, Rousseau. In appearance the *gardian* resembled his cousin of the American Middle West, but his main weapon was the classical trident of Poseidon, a lance about nine feet long topped with a triple-pronged fork (resembling the Italian *lancia* and the gaucho *garrocha*), used for both offense and defense and skillfully employed to deflect the charge of a bull without injuring the animal. He lived in a *cabane*, the windowless walls and roof of dried yellow reeds, and the ridge reinforced against the violent mistral wind. The superb long-maned white horses of the Camargue, of ancient stock, then ran wild before the *gardians* collected and tamed them. These horses inspired some of the finest passages in *Mirèio*, and it is worth while quoting them in the excellent and eloquent translation of the late Roy Campbell, a poet who really lived the life of Véran (and indeed of *Calendau*) in Provence:

> *In the grey wastes of dread,*
> *The haunt of shattered gulls where nothing moves*
> *But in a shroud of silence like the dead,*

THE LION OF ARLES

I heard a sudden harmony of hooves,
And, turning, saw afar
A hundred snowy horses unconfined,
The silver runaways of Neptune's car
Racing, spray-curled, like waves before the wind.
Sons of the Mistral, fleet
As him with whose strong gusts they love to flee,
Who shod the flying thunders on their feet
And plumed them with the snortings of the sea;
Theirs is no earthly breed
Who only haunt the verges of the earth
And only on the sea's salt herbage feed—
Surely the great white breakers gave them birth.
For when for years a slave,
A horse of the Camargue in alien lands,
Should catch some far-off fragrance of the wave
Carried far inland from his native sands,
Many have told the tale
Of how in fury, foaming at the rein,
He hurls his rider; and with lifted tail
With coal-red eyes and cataracting mane,
Heading his course for home,
Though sixty foreign leagues before him sweep,
Will never rest until he breathes the foam
And hears the native thunder of the deep.
But when the great gusts rise
And lash their anger on the arid coasts,
When the scared gulls career with mournful cries
And whirl across the waste like driven ghosts:
When hail and fire converge,
The only souls to which they strike no pain
Are the white-crested fillies of the surge
And the white horses of the windy plain.
Then in their strength and pride
The stallions of the wilderness rejoice;

They feel their Master's trident in their side,
And high and shrill they answer to his voice.
With white tails smoking free,
Long streaming manes, and arching necks, they show
Their kinship to their sisters of the sea—
And forward hurl their thunderbolts of snow.

Still out of hardship bred,
Spirits of power and beauty and delight
Have ever on such frugal pastures fed
And loved to course with tempests through the night.[1]

Ourrias too lived in the Camargue, for his work was allied to and often corresponded with that of the *gardian*. The savage black bulls were the lineal descendants of a great Asiatic breed which centuries ago came westward until they followed the Rhône to its delta, and it was these which Ourrias helped to collect, often by the expedient of using decoying oxen. The *gardians* having driven them into a village square or an enclosure improvised by tying wagons together—this drive was known as an *abrivade*—Ourrias would overcome the bulls by throwing them down by their horns, the "horn wrestling" of Greek origin. Then came the *ferrade* or branding, a violent and primitive operation which had elements of both drama and comedy, when around a fire of tamarisks Ourrias would preside over the ceremony. Afterwards there would be a *cours libre*, the Provençal version of the bullfight, in which, unlike the Spanish *mise à mort*, the bull was unhurt but the *raseteurs* risked being impaled on the beast's lyrelike horns as they tried to pluck the *cocarde* or tassel from the animal's head.

All three suitors are rejected, and Ourrias, angry and sullen, rides away across the stony Crau where he encounters Vincèn. There is a fight in which Ourrias is beaten, but a few moments

1. *Horses of the Camargue* (London, 1936).

afterwards Ourrias treacherously attacks Vincèn with a trident and leaves him for dead in a welter of blood. Ourrias now attempts to cross the Rhône, but it is the Eve of Saint Médard, and on the further shore he sees the procession of the ghosts of all those drowned in the river, all carrying lights and in search of the act of faith which they must make before they can enter Paradise. Whether the tiny boat carrying Ourrias is itself a phantom or whether the ghosts are waiting to claim him is not immediately clear, but the craft goes down and Ourrias is lost. Thus Mistral uses Christian legend and local folk belief to defeat evil. Meanwhile Vincèn is found alive by swineherds and carried to the Mas di Falabrego, where Mirèio's mother insists that he be taken to Taven the witch to have his wounds healed. Vincèn and Mirèio are left alone in the witch's cavern in the hills of the Alpilles, in a labyrinth filled with phantoms and terror and menace in every form. Taven now goes into long supernatural rhapsodies and we are caught up in a nightmare world of witchcraft and black magic, but Vincèn is healed by her incantations. This episode in the underworld, the sixth canto, has a parallel in the sixth canto of Virgil's *Aeneid*.

Vincèn now persuades his father to visit Mèste Ramoun and ask, on the son's behalf, for Mirèio's hand. The two old men then talk it out, though the cautious Mèste Ambròsi does not mention Mirèio by name but refers merely to his son's passion for the daughter of a prosperous farmer. Only when it is clear that the suit would be hopeless does Mirèio herself reveal that she is the girl whom Vincèn loves and that she returns his passion. There follows a scene in which Mèste Ramoun explodes with wrath and the two old men quarrel violently and part in high dudgeon, while Mirèio, also abused and chastised, is packed off weeping to bed. It is the Eve of Saint John, Midsummer night, and the harvesters dance the *farandole* round the blazing log fire, brandishing their shining blades and firing muskets through the flames, while Mirèio lies with a breaking heart.

Mirèio now remembers Vincèn's counsel to go to *Li Santo*, the Holy Maries, and invoke their help whenever she is in trouble, and before dawn, while the household is asleep, she sets out on foot for the shrine of Les Saintes Maries. It is a terrible journey for a young girl, roughly ten leagues, and it takes her two full days. She reaches the Rhône—the Grand Rhône or main branch—on the evening of the first day, and after being sheltered by a fisherman's family she is ferried across the river early next morning in the rosy flush of dawn. Then comes her ordeal, crossing the wastes of the Camargue with its cruel mirage under a pitiless scorching June sun, appealing to Saint Gent as she suffers from thirst. She is smitten with sunstroke and has barely the strength to totter into the church of Les Saintes. She flings herself down before the altar and calls upon the saints:

> O Sànti Mario,
> Que poudès en flour
> Chanja nosti plour,
> Clinas lèu l'ouriho
> De-vers ma doulour!

(Oh Holy Maries, who can change our tears into flowers, hear me in my grief!)

Meanwhile Mirèio's parents having raised the alarm and discovered from an old shepherd that their daughter, murmuring *Li Santo*, had passed that way, had set off in pursuit and now arrived to find her in a state of collapse. She is carried up to the high chapel where the relics of the Saints rest, and she has a vision of the Marys who bring her comfort and strength. At last Vincèn too has crossed the Crau and, grief-stricken, he kneels beside her. The chant rises from the church below, and the Maries appear for the last time to carry her away in the small sail-less boat to Paradise and the contemplation of the beatific vision. While Vincèn and Mirèio's parents weep and lament the chant rises again from below: "If it be peace that they need, then grant them peace."

This, very briefly, is the story of *Mirèio*, yet Mistral stretched it into seven hundred and forty-eight stanzes of seven lines each. For on the slightest pretext he took the opportunity to examine and weave into the narrative the entire complex of Provençal life, history and legend. We have noted his expatiations on the lives of the shepherd and *gardian* and his praise of the Camargue horses, but there is much more. He even manages to introduce a ballad dealing with the naval action which the French Admiral Suffren fought with the English in the Indian Ocean. He brings in the processes of olive cultivation and silk-weaving, and the Mithraic cult of the bull. As we have seen, he touches upon Provençal belief in witchcraft, fairies and evil spirits through the medium of Taven. The Eve of Saint John is an excuse to describe the harvest and its ritual fire dance. When Mirèio dresses for her journey to Les Saintes, her clothes and thus the regional costume are described in some detail. When her parents raise the alarm and send a messenger to question all the laborers of the area there is a picture of the entire farm, for the runner passes from the mowers to the ploughmen, from the ploughmen to the harvesters, and so on, until the herdsmen and the shepherds are reached, all of whose work is described. Finally, when Mirèio invokes the Holy Maries, Mistral puts into their mouths their own history, their persecution in the Holy Land, their long voyage to Provence and their conversion of the country. Yet another digression, a detailed description of the Christmas ceremonies, was originally included in the seventh canto but was omitted. Landscape and topography are brilliantly described and Mistral's sense of place is marked, yet all this is skillfully subordinated to the narrative, and the construction and sense of form are almost flawless.

A common charge levelled against Mistral is a weakness in portraiture, his characters little more than symbols or ciphers. Yet both the old patriarchs Mèste Ambrosi and Mèste Ramoun are modelled on the character of old François Mistral and illustrate various facets of Mistral *père*. We have Frédéric's words for that, for in a letter to Adolphe Dumas he said that he had portrayed his father in these two forms, and that he had not attributed to the two patriarchs anything that he had not seen in his father or heard from his mouth. Both Mirèio and Vincèn are unsophisticated, indeed almost naive, young people, wholly untainted by the Freudian complexes of our own time. Mirèio is a virtuous maiden, her look like dew upon the leaf, sweeter and purer than starlight. Vincèn is without guile, without the seediness of our own fictitious heroes, and if he bears the stains of his humble calling and is burned brown like a peasant 'the black soil to the best vintage will give birth.'

In the entire work there is no trace of literary consciousness or influence, even if Mistral declares at the outset that he is attempting to do what Homer did for Greece. True, there is here the epic tradition of Greece, but the old pagan sensual world is here colored with a delicate Christian mysticism, filled out with the loftier and more sublime sentiments of Catholicism. If there is something of Homer there is also something of Theocritus, while one may recall the treatment of what is an eternal theme in the Greek *Daphnis and Chloe* (a French translation of which, by Paul-Louis Courier, had been available since 1810). Affinities between Mistral and both Sir Walter Scott and Burns have been found. The Scott findings are valid enough if based purely on qualities of local patriotism, but the parallel with Burns is striking. Both were sons of humble farmers, both were sometimes compelled to pose as illiterate ploughmen for a metropolitan audience, both rejected the advice that they should drop the regional idiom and write in the national language, both recreated their native tongue and the local ballads, and both inspired a rare and lasting mystique. Of Burns, Mistral himself in a letter to William Bonaparte-Wyse had this to say:

> I have read the good Robert Burns, and I understand his immense popularity in Scotland. He has all the virtues and failings of the people of whom and for whom he sings, poetic and dreamy, rough and outspoken, strong and convinced of his independence. He skilfully practised realism before the French even knew the word, but the realism of Burns does not shock me like the *Baigneuse*[2] of Courbet. The charm and the secret of Burns lies in his simplicity. May I, like him, clothe my own songs with that divine light.

If the Provençal poets lacked the unity and coherent history and culture that produce a living traditional epic such as Adam Mickiewicz's *Pan Tadeusz*, Mistral by the skillful portrayal of life in a rustic community, from firsthand experience, achieved at least the semblance of such unity and coherence. There is indeed a deal of affinity between Mickiewicz and Mistral, for both wrote poetic pictures of country life, and both wrote to express their proud but wounded patriotism and their political hopes. In *Pan Tadeusz* Mickiewicz portrayed the life of the Polish gentry at the beginning of the nineteenth century, while in *Mirèio* Mistral portrayed the life of the Provençal peasant in the same era; both were written in a Homeric manner, though *Mirèio* has none of the humor of the Polish epic. The true regional writer is a local dedicated patriot, writing to preserve a still existing if declining way of life —Hardy in English Dorset, Gabriel Miro in Spanish Murcia, C. F. Ramuz in the Swiss Valais. Like them Mistral was a regional writer in the best sense.

2. *The Bathers*, a painting by Gustave Courbet (1819-77).

Mistral's first work was a triumph, and there were but a few thin dissenting voices. The Avignon journal *Semaine Religieuse*, for example, declared certain passages to be contrary to Christian morality; the *Revue des Bibliothèques* of the same town said much the same thing and argued that the love of Mirèio and Vincèn was painted too strongly, and two Marseilles periodicals, perhaps under the influence of Victor Gélu, sneered at it. But these were the exceptions amid a tumult of acclaim. On March 12, 1859 a ceremony honoring Mistral and *Mirèio* was held in the convent of the saintly Père d'Alzon in Nîmes, where, in the presence of the Bishop, Père d'Alzon and the *Messieurs de la conférence de Saint-Vincent*, Jean Reboul praised *Mirèio* as being "the most beautiful mirror in which Provence ever saw herself" and garlanded Mistral for his work as *"bon catholique."* On the same day Mistral wrote to Adolphe Dumas supplying some details of his life and work which Lamartine had asked for, and affirming his religious faith and extolling the virtues of his father. Four days later he went to Paris.

This time he stayed for two months in the Rue du Faubourg-Montmartre. It was a new Paris, for three years under the domination of Baron Haussmann, Napoleon's Prefect of the Seine department, had made a difference. Entire areas of medieval slums had been cleared; the Cité was being ringed with spacious boulevards and others were being thrown out in long radiating lines, an ambitious project aiming at both civic magnificence and military strategy. Mistral called at once on Adolphe Dumas and Lamartine. Lamartine had now written his tribute to the young poet, devoting the whole of the fortieth *Entretien* or essay of his *Cours familier de Littérature* to what he entitled *Littérature villageois: apparition d'un poème épique en Provence*. Lamartine in fact read this out to Mistral, perhaps somewhat to the latter's embarrassment, for it referred to "this handsome and modest young man"

73

and went on to praise his manners and bearing and everything else about him.

It was now that, for the first time, Mistral and Alphonse Daudet met. The young Alphonse indeed called on Mistral at his lodgings, for he was delighted to find that *Mirèio* mentioned a *mas* which had belonged to his own family, the Font du Rei at Beaucaire. Daudet was then a struggling journalist, handsome in a dark, almost barbaric manner, with dark eyes and long eyelashes that fluttered, a new immature beard and a thick luxuriant head of hair which covered his neck. Fame was not yet on his horizon, but this meeting with Mistral was perhaps indirectly responsible for inspiring some of his best work. Through Daudet Mistral seems now to have met Barbey d'Aurevilly, the Norman aristocrat and former dandy, a theatrical and flamboyant character, now driven by the loss of his family fortune into poverty and journalism. D'Aurevilly was a staunch Royalist and Catholic who, however, in such works as *Les Diaboliques* was capable of violent oscillations between mysticism and satanism. He was one of those whose tribute to *Mirèio* was now added to a glowing Paris press. Indeed Mistral was already celebrated, and there were jokes about the mistral wind being reincarnated, while others said that the poet's name had shaped his destiny.

It was Easter, and Mistral with Daudet and Dumas were confessed by Père Félix in the Cathedral of Notre Dame, after which they took communion. Daudet in later years seems to have twisted the incident, for in his *Journal*, Edmond de Goncourt, quoting Daudet, says that the communion was followed by a gross feed in which Mistral was tipsy. This is quite unbelievable and must be a figment of Daudet's imagination, for we know how he liked to embroider things with a touch of fantasy. Indeed Mistral in a letter to Paul Suchon nearly half a century later refers to the emptiness in the soul of the unbeliever and recalls how moved he was by the crowds in the cathedral that Easter.

What else Mistral did in those eight weeks is not recorded, for his memoirs, *Moun Espelido,* end with the publication of *Mirèio.* Paris was a noisy gaslit world of pleasure, and if he had little time for this he must have enjoyed the life of *Le Tout Paris,* that part of Parisian life made up of men of letters, journalists, artists and distinguished foreigners who haunted the cafes, restaurants and theatres about what is now the Place de l'Opéra. Perhaps he was taken by friends to two celebrated restaurants specializing in the cuisine of the South—Aux Frères Provençaux in the Rue de Valois, founded in 1786 by three brothers from Marseilles who introduced *bouillabaisse* to Paris, and Noel et Peters, which first introduced *homard à l'Americaine,* of Provençal origin, to the capital. But the glamour and opportunities of Paris did not hold him. He remembered Jean Reboul's counsel before he left his native village. "Do not forget your mother! Do not forget that it was in a farmhouse in Maillane that you wrote *Mirèio* and that there lies all that will make you great." He returned to Maillane on May 20, as the first summer heat set the Alpilles aglow.

In September *Mirèio* went into a second edition, and Mistral dedicated it to his spiritual father Lamartine: "Je te consacre *Mireille;* c'est mon coeur et mon âme . . . I consecrate *Mirèio* to you; it is my heart and my soul, it is the flower of my years. It is a grape of the Crau which, with all its leaves, is offered to you by a peasant."

*　　*　　*

In the summer of 1859 a cultured young Irishman was wandering through the south of France. Born in 1826, he was the son of Sir Thomas Wyse of county Waterford, a leading member of the Catholic Association, and British Minister at Athens in 1849, and the Princess Laetitia, the daughter of Lucien Bonaparte, brother of Napoleon I. This was by no means the first visit of William Bonaparte-Wyse to the country of his ancestors on the

75

distaff side, but it was to be of the greatest significance and was virtually to launch him upon a strange career. He was spending a few days in Avignon when he looked into the window of Joseph Roumanille's bookshop in the Rue Saint-Agricol and saw a slim paperbacked volume with a strange title. He was something of an expert in philology, but here was a language unknown to him. He strode into the shop, sought the proprietor and asked to be enlightened.

"That, monsieur—but that is Provençal!"

The book was, of course, *Mirèio*. Bonaparte-Wyse took it to his hotel and studied it. When he saw that it was published by the bookseller from whom he had purchased it he returned to the shop, where he learned from Joseph Roumanille of the renaissance of Provençal literature and of the Félibrige. Within a few days Bonaparte-Wyse had acquired sufficient Provençal to write to Mistral. Mistral was a little touched by this communication from a young and ardent proselyte, and he made an appointment for Christmas Day. It was a severe winter, but Bonaparte-Wyse was determined to walk all the way to Maillane. There is a heroic, almost an epic quality about this journey on foot in deep snow and freezing winds, as there is in his greeting to the distinguished poet: "Master, I am come to burn the Christmas log with the poet of *Mirèio*. Forgive me for having arrived in such a filthy condition. Of old, people made pilgrimages on foot to see the cells of saints; since the poets are, in my opinion, the saints of our epoch, I have wished to come on foot to offer you the homage of an English pilgrim."

Mistral was much impressed. "I had never seen," he wrote later, "so much simplicity united to such youth and grace, and so much poetry united to so great a degree of independence and common sense." The attraction must have been mutual, for Bonaparte-Wyse was again at Maillane shortly afterwards, and he commissioned the painter David for a portrait of his new friend. This strange Franco-Irish aristocrat, who said of himself that he was "an odd individual, unusual, without doubt feminine and perhaps a little ridiculous," soon became one of Mistral's closest friends. In January, 1860, he wrote an appreciation of the work of the Félibrige in the *Illustrated London News*, and before long he was himself to become a member of the circle and to write poetry in Provençal. Indeed he learned Provençal to such effect that within a few months Mistral, thanking him for some verses, wrote:

> My great, my true poet, thanks for your Pindaric *Noel*. I will repeat a thousand times you have a great fault—you are too modest . . . your august, solemn and limpid poetry should make a sensation in your country. To the witty, the unexpected, the surprising, the piquant, the mordant qualities of Alfred de Musset you join the gravity, the elevation, the magnificence of the Indian poets . . . You will be the happy singer of the modern idea, because you have the genius of universality, the wing-spread of the condor, and the eye of the eagle.[3]

Meanwhile Mistral had begun his next major poem *Calendau* (*Calendal*), for Aubanel in a letter to Ludovic Legré in the middle of 1859 tells of Mistral's three-day visit to Avignon at Corpus Christi and his preparation for the poem.

It was in 1860 that the Emperor and his Empress were feted in Arles on their way to Marseilles. In 1853 Napoleon had married the Spanish countess Eugénie di Montijo. This at least had the blessing of the people. Tutored by Stendhal, praised by Mérimée ("every hair of her a lioness") and loved by Queen Victoria (one recalls her dark stamp of Spanish beauty in the paintings of Win-

---

3. J. Charles-Roux, *William Bonaparte-Wyse* (Paris, 1917), p. 53.

terhalter), she made the court of the Second Empire the most splendid in Europe. Napoleon had not yet enforced any further measures of centralization, but he had alienated the faithful by his Italian campaign and the big business men by his fiscal measures, and he was now compelled to ease the reins he held over parliamentary liberty. The people were breathing freely again, settling down to a new epoch of material comfort, to the pursuit of money and pleasure. The great Paris Exhibition, the opening of the Suez Canal and the setting up of new banks were all symptoms of the new prosperity. Thus the Emperor and his Empress were well received on their southern tour. In Arles they were greeted by a bevy of Arlésiennes in regional costume who offered bouquets, and the leading girl of this 'ballet' recited in Provençal a ten-line tribute in their honor specially written for the occasion by Mistral, who for the sake of law and order had made his peace with the Empire, or so it would seem. It is highly improbable that Mistral would have done this of his own accord, however, and indeed he was asked for such a piece by the *sous-préfet* of Arles. The farandole was danced by men and girls of neighboring villages who as they did so surrounded the imperial carriage. The various small towns of the area sent their municipal councils bearing their respective banners, that of Les Baux with the seven-pointed star of Balthazar, that of Lamanon the blazon of the Saracens, while that of Arles itself sported the lion, the celebrated *lion d'Arles*. Under the banner of Saint George came the *gardians* of the Camargue on their white horses, holding their tridents aloft. A canopied dais was set up in the ancient arena, and there the Imperial Majesties watched the fete.

Mistral's fellow Félibres had also been busy, and this year saw the appearance of Aubanel's *Li Miougrano entreduberto* (*The Cleft Pomegranate*), which, as we have already seen, was inspired by Aubanel's 'Zani' and recorded his passion and grief. Mistral wrote a delightful preface to the book, and Victor Hugo was among the first to send his compliments to Aubanel. In the following year Anselme Mathieu, the vain and frivolous poet of charming trifles, published his *Farandoulo*, which, said Mistral, "tasted like a spoonful of honey." Mistral was now busy on *Calendau*, but he found time for some lyrics and short pieces like that to Notre Dame d'Afrique, written at the request of the Bishop of Algiers.

It was about this time that Mistral was visited by Damase Calvet, the Catalan poet laureate, for literature in Catalonia was then developing in close connection with that in Provence after a similar history and decay. In 1833 a Catalan poet named Bonaventura Aribau published a poem in his native tongue instead of the normal Castilian. That was the beginning of renewed impulse. Catalonia awoke to the possibilities and soon the works of the great Romantics were translated into Catalan. In 1859 the ancient Floral Games or poetic contests were revived and the *sardana* was rediscovered and became the national dance. It was natural then that Calvet should seek out Mistral, and, as we shall see, Mistral was later to seek out the Catalans. In 1861, after Calvet's visit, Mistral wrote his *Ode to the Catalans,* thrusting at tyrants and invaders and denouncing the Albigensians, when the people of Tarascon, Beaucaire, Toulouse and Beziers made a wall of living bodies against their onslaught. This theme was to be embodied in *Calendau* and it reflected his political conscience.

Meanwhile the friendship between Bonaparte-Wyse and the Félibres had ripened, and there is some interesting and amusing correspondence over this period. Bonaparte-Wyse had apparently invited both Mistral and Aubanel to England as his guests, for Aubanel in a letter to the Irishman touches upon this: "To receive your noble hospitality and see England under your guidance would be splendid. I very much wish to see proud England, to know its civilization, its public parks, the gentle rays of its sun; England, land of the most beautiful horses, the most beautiful flowers, the most beautiful women. . . ."

A little later a letter from Mistral to Bonaparte-Wyse referred to the death of Adolphe Dumas while bathing at Dieppe, "like a poet, like a martyr, like a great man, alone, without parents, without friends, in a fisherman's hut with only a few peasant women about him, facing the wilderness of the ocean." During a spell of wintry weather Mistral wrote "In travelling from Cuanna-Grian to Dublin have you seen anything of the sun? Provence has lost him and the Venus of Arles would vote you a kiss if you could send us any news of him." Again Mistral wrote in humorous vein, "I have been reading in the newspapers that your friend Fitzgerald was proposing and opposing amendments in the House of Commons. That is very good, but would it not be better if he came with his fine ship to take the Félibres to Marseilles, to 'Magalouna', or perhaps to Port-a-Bouc, and that he should lead them on a pilgrimage to the Parthenon or Jerusalem? How much wiser you are, you poet. You will return to us with the nightingales and the grasshoppers, and you will see that Provence has still many charms to reveal to you."

On the third anniversary of the publication of *Mirèio*, at Candlemas in 1862, Mistral was feted by the Sisters of the Assumption of Auteuil, under the wing of Père d'Alzon. It was a year notable for the reorganization of the Félibrige, after the Floral Games at Apt, the little hill town of crystallized fruits, in September. The society was now regrouped into seven sections, each of seven members, plus a *capoulié* or leader. The sections were those of Poetry, History, Languages and Archaeology, Music, Painting, Sculpture and Architecture, and Science, while in addition there was now a section of honorary members, enrolling such people as Bonaparte-Wyse, Damase Calvet, the abbé Bayle, Alphonse Daudet and Jean Reboul.

CHAPTER 5

Parisians in Maillane

CHARLES GOUNOD had written to Mistral about the possibility of adapting *Mirèio* as an opera. Gounod had been for some years organist of the church of the *Missions étrangères* in Paris; he had intended to become a priest, but music had won, and he had recently had a crowning success with *Faust*. He now decided to go to Provence to discuss the new project with Mistral and to immerse himself in the right atmosphere and 'décor.' Consequently he arranged to stay at the Hôtel de la Ville Verte in Saint Rémy, where he arrived in March of 1863. From the little shuttered hotel he looked out onto the spacious Place de la République, where at one end was the Ionic portico of a white classical church and at the other a latticed iron calvary. Beyond, awaiting his exploration, were the grandly-named narrow streets which delivered one at length into the picturesque Rue Kléber, then the little square with an arcaded *Mairie*, and finally the tiny Place Favier with its color-washed houses, plane trees and fountain setting off the patrician mansion of Mistral de Montdragon.

Mistral of course would fetch him to the House of the Lizard barely three kilometres away in Maillane. He would show Gounod the life of the farms and the fields, they would take their aperitif or coffee in the Cafe dóu Soulèu, and they would admire the girls of the village in their *coiffes*. "There are my models," Mistral would say, "there is Mirèio." And Gounod would make notes for the benefit of the costumier and wardrobe mistress of his production. Then, perhaps, they called at Roumanille's home, the Mas des Pommiers in Saint Rémy, though Joseph was no longer there for he had recently married his Félibresse Rose-Anais Gras and lived in Avignon.

Gounod in his correspondence tells how they wandered about the countryside picking violets in a warm early spring, how they walked into the Alpilles, "where is the most beautiful mountain valley that you could see anywhere; it is pure Italy; it is even Greece." As if impatient to show the Parisian the glory of his own horizon, Mistral marched him off from Maillane to Les Baux the very day after his arrival in Provence. From Saint Rémy they took the softly climbing road hemmed with rose gardens and silver olives to the Plateau des Antiques. On the edge of it, along a flowering alley, stood the old convent of Saint Paul du Mausolée, which had been a state-owned asylum since the reign of Napoleon I and was kept by the sisters of Saint Vincent de Paul. There were glimpses of the nuns in the Romanesque cloister and the admirable church, partly remodelled on classical lines, the cloister itself fragrant with oleanders, geraniums and roses, while the early summer gardens were filled with stone pines and pink-flowering chestnuts. Nearby stood all that was left of Roman Glanum—two perfect monuments of yellow stone, a triumphal arch and a 'mausoleum' crowned with a Corinthian lantern, both enriched with carvings of Roman cavalry in action, hunting scenes and garlands of fruit and flowers.

They followed the hot, rough, white road to Les Baux, almost indistinguishable from its natural fortress of limestone, not so much a town that had died as a town that defied human occupation, so that its air was one of inquietude and frustration. The narrow climbing Grand Rue was flanked by charnel houses, albeit enriched with Renaissance carvings, and led into a nightmare world of twisted tottering houses with doorways open to the howling wind, some of them on the edge of an abyss. A few living habitations clustered about the little Place Saint Vincent with its welcome shade of elms and nettle trees, the chapel of the Pénitents Blancs and the parish church where the shepherds gathered for the *pastrage* at Christmas. The village street dwindled into a track breaking out with carbuncles of stone and ascending to the high crags and the wilderness. Below lay a vast crumpled landscape where the Crau merged into the Camargue. Gounod was tremendously excited, and perhaps he struggled to visualize how this 'décor' could be brought to the stage. But he was awed too. "The panorama is more vast than that of the Roman Campagna, and terrifyingly stern," he wrote; it was all "a marvel of savagery."

Gounod stayed in Saint Rémy for three months while he worked on his opera, often writing at an open window of the hotel. He discussed it, of course, with Mistral, and told him that the libretto would be by Michel Carré. He was "enchanted" by Mistral, and he wrote to his wife of Mistral's simplicity and essential goodness, as pure and unsophisticated as his poetry. "Je le tiens enfin ce beau et bon Mistral tant rêvé, tant cherché et tant desiré."

While Gounod was preparing to launch his opera in Paris Mistral was working on *Calendau*, and he had also begun the mammoth task of compiling, the *Trésor dóu Felibrige*, which was to be as much an encyclopaedia of Provence as it was a dictionary of the Provençal language. He had, for the time being, made his peace with the Empire, and in August he accepted the Legion of Honor—he was barely thirty-three years of age. He was also actively engaged on behalf of others, though sometimes it must have been with a twinkle in his eye and tongue in cheek. The throne of Greece having fallen vacant, Mistral wrote in August to the editor of the *Siècle* in Paris putting forward the views of the Félibrige as to a candidate. Their candidate was their own royal personage Bonaparte-Wyse. And what better king for Greece than a poet? Mistral submitted these claims brilliantly if extravagantly:

> Near relations and old friends of the Greeks by the marriage of the Phocean Botis with the daughter of Mannus, ancient king of Provence, we have the right by many more titles than anyone else to offer a Prince to the Athenians. Announce, then, as quickly as possible that the only man who can give to Greece guarantees of liberty, glory and happiness, and who is capable of silencing all jealousies, is William Bonaparte-Wyse. . . . He is descended through his fathers from the Kings of Ireland. He knows Greek better than any of the candidates proposed hitherto, and perhaps better than the Academies of Athens, Argos and Corinth. He has translated and commented on Lycophron. That is enough. English, French, Latin, Italian, Spanish and Provençal complete his linguistic repertory. He possesses wealth not to be condemned by a Mediterranean Prince. Then he is a great poet, a man of large heart, and of strong sense, with a passion for the arts and a life of sunshine, so much so that he is capable of restoring to the Greeks the century of Pericles, if that miracle is possible. Finally, he is thirty years of age, he is as handsome as Apollo of Delphi, and he is ignorant of his candidature.[1]

Unfortunately the editor of the *Siècle* replied that he could mention only official candidates. If Mistral was unable "to push his friend into the blue kingdom of Cypris," however, Bonaparte-Wyse "found other crowns in Provence, and poetry made him forget this lost royalty."

Winter brought Alphonse Daudet again to Fontvielle, between

1. *J. Charles-Roux, op. cit., p. 92.*

Arles and Les Baux. Despite Daudet's exploitation of the South he had a genuine affection for his native Midi, and from time to time he stayed with friends of his family named Ambroy who owned the little chateau of Montauban at Fontvielle. He had visited Montauban in 1860 and again for a few days in the winter of 1862-63 on his way to and from Corsica. On both these occasions he had met Mistral at Maillane, but it was now, in this winter of 1863-64, that he really entered into Mistral's circle. Occasionally he would stay with Mistral at Maillane, as he records in his *Lettres de mon Moulin* and his *Trente Ans de Paris*. "Oh, those nights in Mistral's big room at Maillane . . . his bed in one corner, mine in another, and talk without end." And then, perhaps, in the middle of the night they would dress and steal quietly, carrying their boots in their hands, out of the next room where Mistral's mother slept behind a screen, and out into the darkness and the hustling wind of the Rhône valley en route to Avignon; they were both still young and full of high spirits.

Daudet indeed now joined the Félibres, particularly Aubanel, Mathieu and Pierre Grivolas, the painter, in their wanderings and feasts. He would dance the *farandole* on the heaving bridge of boats at Trinquetaille. He would embrace the Arlésiennes while Aubanel chanted his *Vénus d'Arles*:

Sies bello, o Vénus d'Arles, à faire veni fou!

. . . .

Que sies bello! Venès, pople, vénès teta,
A si ben bessoun, l'amour et la beuta.
(Tu es belle, ô Vénus d'Arles, à faire devenir fou!

. . . .

Que tu es belle! Venez, peuples, venez téter
A ces beaux seins jumeaux l'amour et la beauté.)

85

Once, dining with his friends at the Chênes-Verts, the little inn and dansant near Avignon, he took a flying leap from the high terrace to land like an apparition among the startled dancers down below. Another time he jumped into the river near the Pont du Gard simply to find out how deep it was—he could not swim and would certainly have been in grave danger were it not for the aid of a fisherman. They were up to all manner of schoolboy escapades. It was, of course, a robust age, when the blood of humanity had not been watered down by the spiv mentality of our twentieth century. Where today would one find the secretary of the President of the Senate (Daudet), a chevalier of the Legion of Honor (Mistral), a well-known poet and a well-known painter kissing the girls and scandalizing the local landlords and all but arrested by the police, or eating eel stew in a low haunt of the Rhône boatmen in Arles?

Daudet in his published work refers not only to the above but also shows us something of Mistral at this time. Mistral looked like a villager and to a large extent lived the life of a villager. The high collar and stovepipe hat that he wore in Paris were put aside. Now he wore "his felt hat, pulled down over his brows, wearing no waistcoat, but a jacket, with his red Catalan sash round his waist, his eyes lighted up, the glow of inspiration in his cheeks, splendid, but with a genial smile, as striking as a Greek shepherd, striding along, hands in pockets, making poetry."[2] The portrait by Hébert, which was done about this time, gives a clear impression of his noble features, the classical brow and nose, the large brilliant clear eyes, the long mustache and the Imperial beard, like a young "Buffalo Bill."

Madame Mistral had made the House of the Lizard comfortable. The drawing room, hung with a bright wallpaper, contained

---

2. *Lettres de mon Moulin* (Paris, 1869).

a couch with a yellow diamond pattern, two armchairs of straw, and, in the corner by the window, a writing desk filled with old books and dictionaries, while on the mantelpiece were the Venus of Arles and the other armless Venus, over which hung the portrait of the poet by Hébert. On the desk at this time Daudet saw the unfinished manuscript of *Calendau*. Madame Mistral, never at ease with a *Franchiman*, would leave the two men to lunch on roast kid, cheese straight from the mountain, wort jam, figs and muscatel raisins, washed down with a Châteauneuf-du-Pape. The day would be spent discussing *Calendau* and other matters and strolling about the village. Daudet was singularly fortunate, for, so he claims, everything seemed to happen when he visited Maillane. Mistral was now a municipal councillor, and Daudet has related how one morning his friend was serenaded by musicians who brought him an *aubade*, Mistral then drawing the big table into the middle of the drawing-room and placing on it the bottles of *vin cuit* (a rich local wine from the boiled grape, normally reserved for festivals) for the fife players and drummers to drink his health.

On the same day Daudet saw a procession of the Penitents in the village. Interminably, they passed by like spectres, the Pénitents Blancs, Bleus, Gris and Rouges, each in his medieval *cagoule* or gown, the long cloak reaching to the ground and the lofty pointed conical hood covering the entire head and shoulders, with narrow slits for the eyes. With them came the confraternities bearing their furling banners flowing with patterns in rose and gold and chartreuse, and the carved and sculptured saints borne on the shoulders of the faithful or on a mobile dais draped with green velvet and rich fabrics and bouquets of flowers. There was the dancing light of myriads of candles, the chanting of litanies and the pealing of the church bells. There had been Pénitents Blancs in Maillane, and in Avignon they were still numerous and influential, among them Mistral's friends Aubanel and Jules Giéra, while old Monnier, the army sergeant from Africa who worked in Mistral's old school, had been a Pénitent Rouge. The chapels of the Penitents in Avignon were beautiful and intriguing, and that of the Pénitents Noirs at the end of the Rue de la Banisterie (which we noticed earlier) was rivalled by that of the Pénitents Gris, across a footbridge over the Sorgue stream, caught up in the ruins of the Cordeliers' convent with its gilded chapels and wrought iron grilles and lattices.

The procession having passed, the saints were returned to their chapels, and the two friends went to see the bulls and the games. With nightfall there was dancing beneath lighted colored lanterns in the little square outside the Cafe dóu Soulèu. Then they returned to the House of the Lizard for supper and retired to Mistral's room with its two great beds and hardly anything else. "The modest room of a peasant," Daudet called it; even the walls were bare, devoid of paper. When the Academy awarded the author of *Mirèio* a prize of 3,000 francs Madame Mistral suggested that her son should use some of it for papering the walls and plastering the ceiling. Mistral would have none of it. "No, no," he said, "this is the silver of poets, it is not to be touched for such mundane things."

Daudet returned to Paris early in 1864, but he was joined soon afterwards by Mistral, who in March went to Paris for the production of Gounod's opera. *Mireille* opened at the Théâtre Lyrique on March 19. Mistral complained about the hacking of his work and said that he could not recognize his poetry in the opera, but it achieved a limited success. Soon the people were whistling the tunes from it, and this presumably helped to build up both Mistral's popularity and the sales of his work. It was not, perhaps, pure opera, and it was not so much *drame lyrique* or serious opera as it was *dramma per musica* or a play set to music. Something of Gounod's ecclesiastical manner (he was devoutly religious) crept into it, but Emile Zola could not say of it, as he said of *Faust*, that it was "the music of a voluptuous priest." Later critics have dismissed it as romantic folklore and hyperbole, the substitution of "garlands for garlic."

Mistral's friends were at the theatre in strength, and it was there that Mistral with Ernest Daudet, Alphonse's brother, met François Bravay, the 'nabob' of Daudet's novel *Le Nabab*. Bravay was yet another son of the Midi, but he had made a fortune in Alexandria and he now lived and entertained on a fabulous scale in Paris and at his château of Belleau near the nougat town of Montélimar, where a little later Mistral was a guest. Mistral was not long in Paris, for, as he wrote to Bonaparte-Wyse, Paris was a furnace, "nothing so gay as Châteauneuf-du-Pape."

A letter from Aubanel reveals that Bonaparte-Wyse was in Avignon again toward the end of April, and that he was closely followed by the Comte de Séménow. Aubanel gives some details of this Nicholas de Séménow. He was a Russian noble, an admirer of Alfred de Musset, a Francophile and a lover of Provence. He was said to be an 'exquisite' writer in French and had written several novels, the last of which had involved him in a sword duel with a Prince of Palermo in which both combatants were wounded. Mistral wrote de Séménow reprimanding him and inveighing strongly against the practice of duelling. De Séménow built a large villa amid the *chênes-verts* or evergreen oak trees on the Rhône bank outside Avignon, near the restaurant called the Chênes-Verts, a favorite haunt of the Félibres. The villa, itself called the Villa des Chênes-Verts, was designed and decorated in a somewhat Italian style by the brothers Grivolas, with terraces and parapeted galleries. Looking at it today one is a little surprised by Aubanel's dictum that it was in "irreproachable taste."

The villa became another Font-Ségugne, where the Séménows

gave Félibrean banquets and received Spanish refugees. The Countess de Séménow, in a *robe de gaze* "more brilliant than the sun," her blonde hair falling about her shoulders, "more gracious than a fairy," presided over these banquets. In the portrait by Pierre Grivolas she is a tall majestic figure with her hair piled up and studded with diadems, an ample lace collar like a fichu above the low-cut bosom, with one hand resting on the piano and the other holding a fan. She was the godmother of Bonaparte-Wyse, who later married her niece, and Mistral wrote a verse in her honor which was later embodied in *Lis Isclo d'Or*. It was in this year of 1866 that Mistral wrote his celebrated lyric *La Coumtesso* (*The Countess*). While everybody knew that 'the Countess' meant 'Provence' just as 'Cathleen' meant 'Ireland', it is probable that Mistral had the Countess de Séménow in mind when he gave the poem its title and wrote the opening lines: "I know a Countess of imperial race both in rank and beauty, fearing no one high or low, and yet the light of her eyes is veiled with sadness."

The underlying political significance of *La Coumtesso* is, however, quite plain. The Félibrige was at this time flirting with the Catalan poets, and Bonaparte-Wyse, who was always travelling about and was the society's best ambassador, was spreading the Félibrean gospel in Spain, where he had met Victor Balaguer and Quintana. Like Dante, Mistral envisaged a vast Latin federation, and Bonaparte-Wyse was as enthusiastic as the *maître*. There were, of course, marked affinities between the French and Spanish Republicans, between Spanish provincial separatism and the Commune, and between the Carlist cause and that associated with the Comte de Chambord. In September 1866, a delegation of Catalan poets called on Mistral in Maillane, and in January of the following year Mistral accompanied Victor Balaguer to Paris. Balaguer was a brilliant and versatile character, poet, dramatist, novelist, historian and politician, four times cabinet minister, then banished from Spain as a political exile. His Paris mission was to join the Spanish liberals, Mistral's mission was to join the republican opposition and overthrow Napoleon III and set up a Federalist regime in France, possibly with a virtually independent Provence. At least that was the charge, for in some quarters Mistral was now accused of separatism.

Nothing could be further from the truth. In a letter to Bonaparte-Wyse, dated March 1, 1865, Mistral wrote that while they should prepare to accelerate the federal movement he was not given to the stupid idea of separation from France. "Non pas que j'aie l'idée niaise de rêver une séparation de la France. Les temps futurs sont à l'union et non à la séparation. Mais aussi et surtout, ils sont à la liberté, à la liberté des races, des individus, dans l'harmonie." And there is his *Ode to the Catalans* of 1861, in which he said "We men of Provence, one flame, are frankly and loyally part of the great France, as you, the Catalans, are part of noble Spain . . . it is good to be numerous and to be called the children of France. . . ."

From the first he was a regionalist, strong in *esprit de province,* and as such he was opposed to the centralization, the Big Business deals and machine worship of the Empire. He was a dedicated local patriot, and in the new federal idea—only then coming into play in Switzerland and America—he saw the only solution for his Provence. It was the fundamental principle of the sovereignty of the people, and in the federal idea he saw the pattern of governmental organization, civic harmony and political moderation. It seems extremely unlikely that he wanted Provence to be a sovereign state, for there was something of the visionary about him, even though at that time he could not have foreseen what twentieth-century totalitarian greed could do to such small and unprotected "sovereign states."

Equally, he was too far-seeing to be deceived by the fallacy of

Benthamism, and like John Stuart Mill (who now lived in Avignon) if he were a Socialist it was a pragmatic and undoctrinaire socialism that he believed in. It seems difficult to believe in the consistency of his views as he formulated his complex *politik*, yet consistent he was. A measure of disillusionment was inevitable, and he was yet to make his compromise.

CHAPTER 6

The Valiant Fisherman

INDEED MISTRAL may not have gone to Paris on a deliberate political mission at all, and though it is true that he accompanied Balaguer on the journey he seems to have gone for the much more mellifluous purpose of attending a wedding. He was, in fact, witness at the civil ceremony which followed the wedding of his friend Alphonse Daudet to Julia Allard in the church of Saint Denis du Saint Sacrement. Paris was preparing for the International Exhibition, the new Opéra designed by Charles Garnier was rising like a bridal cake, and work had begun on the enormous Palais de Justice on the Ile de la Cité. This was a new Paris of gay crowded boulevards, but such had been the violent criticism of the demolition of old Paris that the architect Baron Haussmann was to be dismissed a few months later.

Again Mistral met Daudet's friends, among them one whom he knew well by repute and indeed may have met earlier, Paul Arène, for Arène was at that time writing Provençal verse for Joseph Roumanille and the *Armana Prouvençau*. Arène was born in Sisteron, the rocky citadel in the mountains above the Durance of Provence, so that like Daudet he was an 'exile' in Paris, dallying in the bohemian cafes and in particular the Café de Madrid, a haunt of Daudet and a center of subversive activity, and the

Café Voltaire, where he was later to take part in the foundation of the Paris branch of the Félibrige. Anatole France has described "son visage immobile [qui] semble avoir été taillé dans le buis d'un bois sacré par un chevrier aimé des dieux, au temps des faunes et des dryades," and there is a delightful caricature of him by André Gill, reproduced in *Les Nouvelles Littéraires* of November 17, 1928, which shows him in a cockaded hat riding a winged insect with a quill in his hand. Like Daudet, he was a gentle and humorous painter of Provençal manners, and, as we shall see, much of the credit for Daudet's *Lettres de mon Moulin* is rightly his.

The Daudets spent their honeymoon in the Midi, where they stayed at Montauban again and visited Maillane and met the poets of the Félibrige, Julia for the first time. Julia Daudet even made attempts to read *Mirèio* in the original Provençal, and since she was now in Mirèio's native terrain she glimpsed some of the beauty and wonder of the poem. Now there was also *Calendau* to read, for it was published at last, and in the previous autumn Daudet had given it some advance publicity in an article in the new paper *Evénement* on *Le Livre de l'hiver prochain* (later included as *Le Poéte Mistral* in *Lettres de mon Moulin*).

Calendau is the story of a country delivered from tyranny by the heroism of one of its sons, a simple fisherman of Cassis. It is rich in symbolism and in the glorification of civic virtues, and it reflects Mistral's political temper at this time. It may well be that it is a finer poem than *Mirèio*, but it never captured the public imagination as *Mirèio* did; it was too learned for that, too weighty with philological and historical considerations, too impassioned in its barely disguised plea for political sovereignty. It was again a story of Provence, but its hero and heroine were unreal, remote, little more than symbols. Calendau and Esterello could not touch the heart as Vincèn and Mirèio had done. The story, inspiring though it is, is hardly convincing, for where—let alone in Provence where the course of true love hardly ever ran smoothly and lovers were hedged about by the pride and greed of patriarchs and matriarchs—where would a simple fisherman wed a countess who was the last heiress of the great House of Les Baux, reputedly descended from Balthasar himself, and whose ancestors included Emperors of Constantinople and Princes of Orange? For such Esterello was, and to complicate matters further she was already married to the Count of Les Baux, though the marriage had never been consummated. (Mistral seems, incidentally, to have endowed Esterello with some of the traits of the Countess de Séménow, though hers was a happy marriage.)

The Count Severan, however, turns out to be a bandit, and Esterello flees from him by night to take refuge in a mountain cave. Calendau, having somehow heard of this, crosses Provence and finally encounters Severan, whom he provokes with a somewhat bombastic account of his own history and prowess. "I am from Cassis, by the sea," he begins. This is the pretext for Mistral to describe the fishing industry of Cassis in detail. But this is merely a beginning. Now comes, from the lips of Calendau, a presumably uneducated peasant, a dissertation on the authentic history of Provence, its arts and civilization, of the coming of Christianity and the great age of prosperity when it "attained a degree of political independence, of literary culture, of religious tolerance, of elegant custom and of material prosperity, superior to the general condition of the rest of Europe," and finally of the Albigensian invasion from the north, which Mistral vehemently condemns.

Calendau then tells of his love for Esterello and of her haughty rejection of him, but he is determined to win her by deeds of valor and strength. First, he embarks on a fishing expedition, made fabulous and fascinating in the descriptive detail. He nets some twelve hundred tunny fish and buys gold and jewels for Esterello with his gains. She, however, rejects them and shows him the vanity of mere riches; these are not enough, and she quotes the more exalted courtship of the Troubadours. There is a great deal of casuistry in Mistral's treatment of the succession of feats performed by Calendau to please his love, in her rebukes, her direction of his conduct and her sense of right and wrong.

There follows a description of Cassis *en fête*, with traditional jousting and the Provençal dances, all described in detail—the *Farandoulo*, the *Courdello*, the *Pastourello*, the *Mouresco*, the *Triho* and the *Ouliveto*. In a note on these dances and the allied rituals of daily life Mistral observed that ". . . our fathers excelled in clothing life with poetry. This idealization of daily labor . . . contributed not a little to making each one love the condition, and the country into which God had caused him to be born." Calendau then competes in the joust, derived from the Greek water games known as *naumachia* and still practiced on the Provençal coast, though its barbarities have been mitigated. The protagonists face each other on floating platforms raised high above the water and drawn by multi-oared barges, or on platforms mounted high at the stern end of small boats; they are armed with long lances and as they collide they attempt to overthrow each other. Calendau fought his contest at the end of the eighteenth century. Let him speak in the translation of Roy Campbell.[1]

> Up on the tintennes (the tiny platforms) which swing, we were jousting in the finals, and one heard the lances resounding on the wooden plastrons—bang!—at the risk of bursting men's hearts and lungs. Blood streams down from hairy chests, and groaning like water-rails many jousters tumble upside down into the sea. A captain from Ceyrests (a fine place, whoever goes there, they say, remains for good), a

---

1. *Light on a Dark Horse* (London, 1951), p. 278.

sea captain, young and sturdy, had newly returned from the colonies where, in his hatred against tyrants, he had gone to Virginia to fight against the English for liberty. This Captain Negrel had returned on account of being wounded by a musket ball which was lodged in his shoulder. But one day he heard the stirring roll of the kettle drum through his window. He asked his wife, who was looking out, what it was all about. "At Cassis," she said, "they are about to begin the jousts"—"The jousts," he cried, "O Holy Saints of the Camargue! Here we come!" In a flash he had leaped out of bed: neither the tears nor the embraces of his young wife could restrain him. She herself, Rousseline, ran after him (the lovely ardent girl), pleading and scolding him tenderly for his madness. But great danger begets great valor. Negrel, like a lion, had entered the ranks of the jousters: and while the others shocked and hurtled even to very death, Rousseline and her sisters, almost fainting, wept by the shore and recited the hymn of Our Lady of La Ciotat; "Three girls of La Ciotat went out one fine morning to pray to the beautiful Crowned Virgin, but did not find her on the altar." They stopped, terrified by the thunder of the shocks of shields and lances. Then they continued—"but they saw Our Lady, all soaking wet, in the distance, returning from the sea". But now the uproar of the people drowned their song because a terrible antagonist was rushing upon Negrel like a Spanish bull. It was the unbeatable Alpheran! He was redoubtable, because of the unfair way in which he abused his great strength. Jousters usually hold their lance to the shoulders. Not so Alpheran. With one hand stretched out catching the other's lance he precipitated his adversaries into the water, defying the terrified umpires. Many had already drunk of the salt wave—even Granthalme who, upright on the platform, had promised to Saint Elmo a beautiful carven boat if he was saved from the number of the vanquished; he fell all the same; Genez and Mitre from Martigues; L'Infernet (or 'Hell-

fire Joe') the Toulonais, a human thunderbolt, who none the
less had been somersaulted, furiously swearing, into the sea:
and so many others besides, disgusted at swelling the list of
the defeated.

With his left arm in a sling, now approached the good
Negrel. Who had foreseen the unlucky encounter—? His
wife, oh yes, for sure, she had had a presentiment because
she went on singing with her sisters—"O beautiful crowned
Virgin, whence do you come so wet from the sea? I come
from the high seas where a sinking ship called for my help,
and, except for the bo'sun, who denied my Son, I've saved
them all."

Then the girls, who had been singing the hymn, fell silent.
Alpheran headlong hurtled at Negrel: the iron on the lance
of Alpheran cracked and split the plastron of Negrel, piercing right through. A cry arose: "Lovely Crowned Virgin."
With his legs upright, the captain fell upside down but so
terribly hurt, and by such a shock, that he sank, like a corpse
sinks into its grave, down to the bottom.

Trembling with fright we saw that Rousseline had fainted.
. . . Divers fished out Negrel . . . they gave him artificial res-
piration and made him come to. The poor girl meanwhile
was out of her mind and wished to die; she almost went off
her head, alas! . . . but a fortnight hadn't passed before Our
Crowned Lady had miraculously cured both of them properly
and given back the lover to the beloved. (Calendau goes on
describing his victory.)

"Now, Alpheran! It's my turn, strike me hard! I haven't
had my say yet!" From his side now he poised, and I from
mine: in our fury and enthusiasm they made us pass almost
out of tackling range.

All the surrounding crowds held their breath. Stung to the
quick with emulation, by God! we came abreast. The oars-
men in their double ranks, almost fagged to death, and row-
ing raggedly, suddenly gave a smart pull. I yelled out. Al-

pheran taken by surprise loses both his head and the terrific
suddenness of his wrist. We were now in equal lance-length:
and each hit one fairly on the other's chest with a great shock
which drove the boats apart. The two lances bend. They
crack. Go on, battering-ram, against the walls! Together
they crack like stalks of hyssop. I found myself hanging to
the ladder. He, the other, had gone tail over tip. Drums and
steel cymbals acclaimed me the victor. In their boat under
the awning of the foresail, the three Prudhommes in con-
sultation awarded and crowned me with the laurel—my Father, with tears in his eyes, was in the midst of the three.
Then altogether all the finalists sang together walking
round the town behind me—"Calendau has won the jousts."

Having emerged victorious, Calendau relates his exploit to Esterello. This time she is impressed, but she teases him with what
she considers a greater feat—the battle fought by Guillaume au
Court Nez against the Saracens and named after the celebrated
Alyscamp cemetery of Arles. Calendau goes off in a bad humor,
such a bad humor in fact that he cuts down all the larch trees on
Mont Ventoux. He is a veritable Hercules, this Calendau, and
returns to boast to Esterello of his achievement, presenting her
with honey which he had taken from the almost-sacred hives of
the Rocher du Cire in the Nesque valley. She berates him soundly
for misusing his strength in such a destructive manner. In expia-
tion he makes the pilgrimage to the Sainte Baume, the cave of
Mary Magdalen. There he meets rival parties of the Compagnons
du Tour de France, the representatives of ancient trades who make
their supplications *pour la Provence catholique*. He prevents their
coming to blows and reconciles them. Esterello is now delighted
and moved and declares her love for him. To preserve his love and
ardor undimmed, however, she sets him one task more, to rid the
country of the monstrous bandit Marco-Mau, which, of course,

he does, for Calendau is an epic hero, a man of destiny, a symbol of Provence's glory.

We have reached the ninth canto, in which Calendau leads Marco-Mau in chains through the city of Aix, where the fisherman is feted like a prince—the fairy tale aspect again—against the background of the traditional pageant of Fête Dieu (Corpus Christi). This pageant, created by King René, is a strange saturnalia of the sacred and the profane, in which Herod and the Devils are 'baited' with long forks, while the Queen of Sheba comes in one chariot and Jupiter, Juno, Venus and Cupid in another. The Count Severan, enraged by Calendau's discourse on love, lures him to his castle where he taunts him and then locks him up in a dungeon. Severan then sets out to capture Esterello, but Calendau escapes to join her and awaits Severan's assault. The narrative ends melodramatically as Severan and his robber band are engulfed in a forest fire, while some two thousand inhabitants of Cassis stamp out the flames and save the lovers.

There are so many objections to the plausibility of the entire story that it might be dismissed as a series of fables were it not for the brilliant passages of poetry and the wealth of imagery, symbolism and folklore. There is not the unity and coherence of *Mirèio*, nor is there the humanity, or at least the revelation of human character, of *Mirèio*, and while Mistral ingeniously and rewardingly weaves into the story an enormous slice of Provence —far more than the Rhodanie of *Mirèio*—one is perturbed by and even incredulous, of Calendau's immense journeys on foot within short spaces of time, from Castellane to Cassis, across mountain and plain, and even by boat, cresting the Mediterranean and passing the Islands of Gold and what is now the Côte d'Azur, "where the wave fringes the golden beach with silver."

Yet despite everything *Calendau* is a remarkable achievement. Indeed it is virtually a national hymn by token of its great invocation:

Pèr la grandour di remembranço
Tu que nous sauves l'esperanço . . .

'By the grandeur of your memories, you who preserved our hopes, you who despite death and the grave fire our youth with even hotter blood than their fathers, you who inspired the troubadours and then made the voice of Mirabeau roar like the mistral; for the waves of the years with their storms and fears in vain merge race and frontiers, for nature and the earth, our mother, will feed her children with the same milk; her breasts always give the good oil to the olive tree. Soul eternally reborn, joyful, noble, aware, breathing in the Rhône waters and in the wind of the Rhône, great spirit of the music-filled woods and of the sun-drenched bays, sacred spirit of my country, I invoke thee!'

Aubanel was prophetic when he declared that if *Mirèio* was the fruit of Mistral's youth then *Calendau* would be the fruit of his manhood. It may not have reached the people in the way that *Mirèio* did, but its broad robust pattern, its drama and color tempted Bizet to write an opera for it; the libretto was to be by Paul Ferrier, but it was finally abandoned since Du Locle of the Paris Opéra-Comique was unsympathetic.

This year 1867 was also notable for the many princely banquets given by the Félibrige and by Bonaparte-Wyse. The Irishman was not only something of a wag, originating Félibrean customs and rites and setting up a kind of inner circle called the 'Society of Arquins'—jolly fellows or 'cards'—but was also a generous host. On May 30 he gave a three-day series of banquets to the Provençal and Catalan Félibres, of whom the chief guest was Victor Balaguer. The first was held in the Hôtel du Louvre at Avignon, now owned by Anselme Mathieu who had turned innkeeper. The feast was laid out in the old Salle des Templiers, the medieval Gothic refectory of the Knights Templars (which today has a mournful restored Viollet-le-Duc appearance), with its clustered columns and great traceried cathedral-like window. Another was held at Font Ségugne and yet another at Vaucluse. The Font-Ségugne banquet was quite an affair. Walls and columns were draped with the arms and colors of Provence and Catalonia, with silk embroidered banners and medallions bearing the names of all the illustrious writers in the *langue d'oc*, crowned with green laurels. The dinner was Lucullan in quantity and quality and the dishes, all needless to say regional, were prepared by the Provençal chef Caire. There were seven courses—the sweet course alone comprised fourteen items—a dozen wines, including those of Frigolet and Châteauneuf-du-Pape (which figured on the menu as *Vin di Félibre*), coffee and liqueurs. In the salon Mistral and Roumanille sat, as they always did, on the chairs which they had occupied from the beginning, chairs of which the seats were covered in old tapestry, and it was said that they would not relinquish those particular chairs for anyone. Then there were speeches, an address by Provençal students from Paris, and the dancing of the farandole, in which the youth of the village of Châteauneuf-du-Gadagne took part, led by Bonaparte-Wyse's wife, the former Ellen Prout.

It was at one of these banquets, at Saint Rémy, during this year that the Coupo Santo made its first appearance. This gilded chalice-like cup supported by stylized figures was presented by the Catalan patriots to the Provençal poets in recognition of the hospitality given to Victor Balaguer. Balaguer declared nobly that in former times Provence and Catalonia exchanged their troubadours and their destiny, and that the same waves which broke against the rocks of the Chateau d'If[2] whitened with their foam the reefs of Montjuich.[3] The inference of course was that Proven-

2. The island fortress off Marseilles.
3. The fortified hill on the edge of Barcelona.

çaux and Catalans were brothers. Mistral responded as only Mistral could. He replied with a lyric, *La Coupo*:

> "*Prouvençau, veici la coupo*
> *Que nous vèn di Catalan:*
> *A-de-reng beguen en troupo*
> *Lou vin pur de noste plant!*
>
> *Coupo santo*
> *E versanto,*
> *Vuejo à plen bord,*
> *Vuejo abord*
> *Lis estrambord*
> *E l'enavans di fort!"*

(Provençaux, here is the cup brought to us by the Catalans. One by one let us drink from it the wine of our own growth. Sacred and plenteous cup, pour out abundantly the enthusiasm and vitality of the strong!) The lyric, for there are more verses, always sung with the same refrain, has become a famous song and almost a national anthem in Provence, and the cup is still treasured by the Félibrige and used at banquets.

Early the following year Balaguer, who by the fluctuations of Spanish politics was now restored to his native Barcelona, invited Mistral and some of the Félibres to Spain, chiefly in order to return their hospitality. Mistral, now sensitive to rumors of his alleged separatism, attempted to persuade an influential and highly-respected body to make up his party. Despite a further fall in the reputation of the Emperor, who barely a year ago had bungled the Mexican adventure and virtually brought about the murder of his protegé the Archduke Maximilian of Austria, Mistral did not wish the Spanish visit to be misinterpreted as another political demonstration. Roumanille, Aubanel and Daudet claimed to have

prior engagements; Gaston Paris (one of the foremost medieval-
ists of the century) refused outright, but Paul Meyer, a scholar of
international repute, Louis Roumièux, another Provençal poet,
and Bonaparte-Wyse (despite the fact that he was awaiting the
birth of his first child) agreed to go. At the beginning of May they
set out from Perpignan in the *diligence* for the Spanish frontier,
where they were received with warmth by a delegation of poets.
At Figueras, where old François Mistral had fought with the
Grande Armée, Mistral had a Mass celebrated in his father's memory, and later he recited his *La Brassado* or *Ode to the Catalans*,
celebrating the unity of the two peoples. They then travelled in
the Queen's own carriage by a special train to Barcelona, where
they were received by a Government deputation and feted with
banquets and flowers which were repeated at the Floral Games.

Before returning home the party visited a number of places in
Catalonia, notably the Catalan national shrine, the Benedictine
monastery of Montserrat on its sacred mountain, perhaps the
Montsalvat of Parsifal, the inaccessible and mysterious resting
place of the Holy Grail, its pale ochre-colored rocks shaped into
incredible fingers, flutes, domes and sphinxes. It was there, on
May 7, that he wrote his tribute *Pèr Nosto-Damo de Mount-Ser-
rat*, the Virgin who dwells in the golden brilliance of the tiny
camarin above the high altar of the basilica. He knelt on the bare
stones and poured out his heart to Her. His youth was over, he
said, and he was already a little weary of earthly travail; his life
was nothing but trouble, his achievements as insubstantial as
smoke, and he begged Her to lead and guide him as a mother. He
returned to Maillane, however, with federation still ringing in his
brain, and that autumn he wrote to Quintana saying that if those
of Spain's noblest men who believed in the federation solution
could achieve their country's liberty by setting up such a regime
the rest of Europe would be in their debt. Tortured Spain was not
to find such a solution, and Mistral was to find his elsewhere.

Meanwhile it was quite a year for Bonaparte-Wyse, for in addition to the birth of a son and the splendor of his banquets, his first volume of poems in Provençal now appeared—*Li Parpaioun Blu* (*Blue Butterflies*). Its success may be gauged by the tributes from such friends and distinguished contemporaries as Victor Hugo, Théodore de Banville, François Coppée and Alphonse Daudet. The last, thanking Bonaparte-Wyse for a complimentary copy, wrote, "Your butterflies are indeed the most beautiful butterflies that I have seen in my life. Since they have arrived with their tiny wings all drunk with the sun our little room is filled with warmth, with perfume and with bright flashes of blue." The *Armana Prouvençau* in announcing the book eulogized the author as "a poet, an ardent, rapturous, exuberant poet." "Since Richard," said Mistral, "since Richard the good King of England, who, when a prisoner in Austria, gave vent to his grief in Provençal, there has been no Englishman, no foreigner of any country who sang so nobly in our tongue." (But this could now be said, with even greater emphasis, of the late Roy Campbell.) These poems are images, fleeting impressions, sketches and songs of the simple joys of nature; there is melancholy in *Thoughts of a Summer Night*, lyricism in *The Fisherwoman*, a noble epigraph in *A Child of Beaucaire*, a certain power in *The Bridge of Avignon*, and there is all the patriotism of the Félibrige in *The Wine of the Félibres*. Whatever the faults of these verses their dexterity and finesse in a difficult language are entirely praiseworthy, and if they are sometimes a little facile, sometimes a little forced, they are as pleasing as spring flowers. Today we may detect a hint of Eighteen-Ninetyishness, a little of Arthur Symons, though strangely enough this Victorian if Irish troubadour never appeared in *The Yellow Book*. His sister, who by her third marriage became Madame de Rute, was a well known writer of French novels; she was not recognized as a Bonaparte by Napoleon III and had to leave France.

Early in the following year, 1869, Lamartine died, and Mistral wrote an Elegy which was later included in *Lis Isclo d'Or*. Lamartine, was 'the great source of pure poetry,' 'the high priest of Adonis, the generous heart,' 'the noble orator and apostolic voice, the great citizen.' He was the overwhelming sun . . .

> *Quand l'heure du déclin est venue pour l'astre,—*
> *sur les collines envahies par le soir, les pâtres—*
> *élargissent leurs moutons, leurs brebis et leurs chiens;—*
> *et dans les bas-fonds des marais—tout ce qui*
> *grouille râle en braiment unanime:—"Ce soleil était*
> *assommant!"*

There is little doubt that the treatment of the old man by the Church—which had not only condemned his work but had opposed the marriage to his niece Valentine de Cessiat and had offered no charity when he was heartbroken by the death of his daughter in the East—had tested Mistral's faith. When Lamartine knew that the end was in sight Mistral wrote him a letter in which he remarked pointedly, "Happily, there is a God and there are inevitable compensations up there."

Indeed Mistral seems to have had his sorrows over this period, mostly occasioned by friends. Bonaparte-Wyse writing from England said woefully that he was ill and at the point of death. "*Moriturus te salutat!* I do not expect to be an inhabitant of this earthly sphere after seven days more . . . I would like to be buried near you, in your field, in sight of your Alpilles. I charge you to keep an eye on your little godson."[4] The little godson was, of course, Bonaparte-Wyse's child, Lucien William Frederic Victor, now almost a year old. But Bonaparte-Wyse's end was not yet. And now there was cleavage within the Félibrige itself, a painful business

4. J. Charles-Roux, *William Bonaparte-Wyse*, p. 193.

for Mistral, who now saw his oldest friends Roumanille and Aubanel bitterly opposed forever. Little is recorded of this breach and there seems to have been no specific reason for it; nothing, that is, beyond the differences in class and temperament of the two men. Such differences, however, were common in an organization where a cousin of the emperor (Bonaparte-Wyse) hobnobbed with a laboring peasant (Tavan), for the Félibrige was above distinctions of rank, creed and politics, and there were Socialists and Royalists as there were Protestants and Catholics. But whatever the cause of the feud it was bitter, and each blamed the other. Roumanille in a letter written at this time says "Our relations have taken such an unfortunate turn, and I don't know quite why, that for a month now Aubanel has failed to visit me and ignores me." A week later Aubanel wrote to another friend, "I have recently suffered one of the most bitter griefs I can remember. A friend of a lifetime, a friend who has been like a brother to me, has tossed me aside in the most paltry and painful manner." Aubanel went on to quote from a sonnet of anger he had written "To a traitor," in which he said he had locked his door forever against his former friend, referring to him as an uncouth dog and an evil-smelling animal. The two were irreconcilable. Even the gentle and discreet Mistral could do nothing to bring them together.

Daudet had now scored a success with his *Lettres de mon Moulin*. It was a stroke of genius on Daudet's part to pretend that these 'letters' or tales were written in an old Provençal windmill, in "a little whitewashed chamber, low and vaulted like the refectory of a convent." They were in fact almost all written in Paris, but there *was* a windmill on the edge of Fontvielle which Daudet knew intimately and loved. Today there are on the outskirts of that village, on the hillside sprigged with pine and oak, a group of rickety windmills crowning the rocky bluffs like drunken giants. They are all derelict save one, which has a restored conical roof and sails and its original wooden machinery of 1814, the various parts of which are now named in cut Provençal lettering. This Moulin de Saint Pierre has become a Daudet museum, the old bolting room filled with the writer's manuscripts, photographs and personal bric-a-brac. Daudet knew all the millers of the district and he would visit each of the mills, there to look through the miller's telescope and to watch the grain being weighed and washed and then spread out on the red-paved floor in front of the mill before being ground between the great millstones. But his favorite mill was the Moulin Tissot, and this was the symbol of the *Lettres*.

Despite the charge against Daudet that he exploited the Midi and caricatured his brethren of the south for the amusement of the Parisians, he had a genuine affection for Provence and Languedoc and his sympathies with and admiration for Mistral and the Félibrige were real and lasting. Though a few of the stories in the *Lettres* concern other places like Chartres, Corsica and Algeria, the book is almost wholly a tribute to Provence. Indeed there is as much of Provence in Daudet's *Lettres* as there is in Mistral's *Mirèio*. There is a spiritual kinship between the two works. Both describe the same region of Rhodanie, from Avignon to the Camargue, from Arles to Les Baux, from the Rhône to the Alpilles. Both are filled with that transparency of intense light, with the heat of the southern sun, with the scent of thyme and lavender, with the song of the cigala and the bleating of the vast flocks of sheep returning to the *mas* from the mountains. Both are filled with the history of Provence, with the glory of its memories, with the lives of its people.

The *Lettres* originally appeared in the Paris papers *Evénement* and *Figaro*, and we have seen that the piece on Mistral was originally published under another title to give advance publicity to *Calendau*. One of the most celebrated of these stories, however,

The Curé of Cucugnan, was virtually stolen from the *Armana Prouvençau* and was the work of Roumanille. Or so it seemed, but on the appearance of Daudet's French version, taken from Roumanille's Provençal, a certain Blanchot de Brenas came forward and claimed that the story was his, originally written in French in a provincial newspaper. Daudet seems to have escaped lightly while Roumanille bore the brunt of de Brenas's complaints and accusations of plagiarism.[5] Another sketch in the *Lettres, Les Etoiles* (*The Stars*) was adapted from an article by Mistral in the *Armana*, and these notes of Mistral's on folklore were reprinted in Mistral's memoirs.

If this seems bad enough there was far worse to come, for later a first-class storm blew up between Daudet and Paul Arène, who claimed to have written a substantial number of the stories in the *Lettres*. The evidence[6] that Arène had a hand in this work is irrefutable, and Daudet ultimately conceded as much, implying however, that Arène was concerned only in those few stories originally signed "Marie-Gaston," indicating a joint authorship, whereas Arène claimed a hand in something like half of the stories. Those who are interested may well discover something of Daudet's debt to Arène in the latter's novels *La Chèvre d'Or, Le Midi rouge* and *Jean des Figues* (described by Charles Maurras as a perfect specimen of French prose), and in his posthumously published *Contes de Provence*. Anatole France placed Arène with Maupassant as a master of the short story, and Vaudoyer called him a classic among Romantics and a spiritual brother of Sterne and Heine.

All this we forgive Daudet for his brilliant evocations of the

5. The matter was fully dealt with by Camille Pitollet in the *Mercure de France*, February 1, 1914.
6. The controversy has been much debated in the French press, and the evidence is admirably summed up by G. V. Dobie, *Alphonse Daudet* (Nelson, 1949).

land of Mistral, for those gems *The Elixir of Father Gaucher, The Three Low Masses* and *The Pope's Mule,* a Provençal version of which appeared in the *Armana* for 1870.

BOOK THREE

Sacred and Profane

For God mingles not with man; but through Love all the intercourse and converse of God with man, whether awake or asleep, is carried on.

PLATO

. . . We outlaws, the children of Eve, do weep and wail the bitterness and tediousness of the day of this present life, short and evil, full of sorrows and anguishes; where a man is oftentimes defiled with sin, encumbered with passions, unquieted with dreads, bounden with cares, busied with vanities, blinded with errors, vexed with temptations, overcome with delights of the world . . .

THOMAS A KEMPIS

Vice and virtue are to the artist materials for an art.

OSCAR WILDE

We live in the belief that we are the masters of our own lives, and that they were given us for enjoyment. That is frankly absurd.

TOLSTOY

CHAPTER 7

Penitential Psalm

AFTER THE Polish and Mexican *débâcles* and the adventure in Italy, Germany resented the dominance of France in European affairs, and both Bismarck and the Empress Eugénie (who had extended her influence to politics) were now intent on war. The famous telegram from Ems (the publication of Bismarck's dispatch), the answer to French protests against the candidature of a German prince for the vacant throne of Spain, was the final insult. On July 19, 1870, France went to war. The confident boast of Leboeuf, the Minister of War, "We are absolutely ready to the last gaiter-button," was soon proved to be fallacious. Indeed there was a deficiency not only in gaiter-buttons but in everything else— money, food, tents, harness, cooking utensils, guns, ammunition, medical supplies, stretchers, to mention only a few items. The railways were inadequate to convey the 300,000 men available for service to the frontiers, and the composition and administration of French regiments was such that Alsatians had to travel to Bayonne and the men of the Midi to Brittany in order to join their units. The result was chaos. The Paris crowds who had frenziedly cried "À Berlin" soon fell silent as one crushing defeat followed another. Soon the Prussians were besieging Paris, and there was a provisional government in Bordeaux. The people of the capital starved and resentment against the Empire smouldered into a bitter hatred.

Mistral in the seclusion of Maillane was deeply shocked by the war, but it is difficult to gauge his true feelings at this time. Certainly the suspension of all social life and activities brought about by the emergency must have driven him more within himself. The young men of the village had gone, and he saw little of his fellow Félibres. The pattern of his political aspirations too is obscure. On September 18 he was suspended from the municipal council of Maillane—he was not to be restored until the beginning of 1878—and it is difficult to see why, especially since his Carlist friend Scipion Doncieux was Prefect of Vaucluse at that time. Certainly he was ranging himself more and more on the side of law and order, and in a letter to Tavan dated November 28 he said that France did not wish to be governed by the Jacobins, the extreme revolutionary party, who were "a hundred times greater tyrants than the Royalists." It was then that he wrote his *Saume de la Penitènci* or *Penitential Psalm*, a cry of shame, despair and horror at France's predicament, a cry of contrition, a kind of *mea culpa*:

> *Segnour en guerro em' en discordi . . .*
> *Segnour, avèn, leissant à reire . . .*
> *Segnour, se la Ciéuta rebello . . .*
> *Segnour, espargno la Provènço . . .*
> *Segnour, voulèn deveni d'ome . . .*

Lord, we have turned our backs on the old ways and laws, and we have destroyed the virtues and traditions of the home.

Lord, we have transgressed, and like pagans we have closed your churches and mocked at your Christ.

Lord, we have denied your commandments and sacraments, and like brutes we live only for ourselves and place our trust in Progress.

Lord, France and Provence have sinned; forgive us our trespasses, for we repent our wickedness.

Lord, we would become men. Set us free. We are Gallo-Romans and gentlemen, and walk erect in our land.

Meanwhile, the war had its repercussions in Rome, where Tavan was a member of the French garrison. On the outbreak of war the French troops were withdrawn from the Holy City, and in September the army of Victor Emmanuel entered the city. Within a few weeks the Papal States were annexed to the Italian kingdom, and thus, after an existence of over eleven hundred years, the temporal power of the Papacy came to an end. Pius IX refused with firm dignity to make terms with the Italian sovereign and showed his independence and spirit by proclaiming within the year the doctrine of Papal Infallibility.

Mistral's friends were temporarily scattered. Tavan now back from Italy was serving somewhere in France. Gounod had fled into exile, to London. Bonaparte-Wyse too was in England. Daudet, like Bizet, was serving with the National Guard in Paris. Echoes of the horrors of the siege of Paris reached Mistral in letters from friends. One from Daudet, dated December 31, was sent by balloon and written in Provençal so that if it fell into the hands of the 'barbarians' they would not be able to read it: "It is cold, it is dark; we eat horse, cat, camel, hippopotamus (ah, if only we had the good onions, the *catigot* and *cachat* of Trinquetaille!). The guns scorch the fingers. Wood is rare. The relieving armies of the Loître do not come. . . ."

With the fall of Sedan and the capture of the Emperor the war was over, and on January 28, 1871 the government of Paris capitulated in the name of France. The cost was tragic in many ways and not least in the cessation of Alsace and one third of Lorraine to Prussia. Daudet in a moving and powerful short story, *The Last Lesson*, has shown us the state of things in Alsace, where the native language was now banned in favor of German. Nor was there yet any real peace for France. In Paris the clamor of elements of insurrection grew ever louder and more violent, and soon the capital was in the grip of the Communards. There was the slaughter of what virtually was civil war. The old cry *Aux barricades* went up again, but the insurgents had overlooked the fact that Napoleon and Baron Haussmann had driven their great boulevards through the city in order to make such guerilla action almost impossible, and thus the rebels were perpetually outflanked and defeated. Nevertheless, the resistance was violent enough. The Tuileries, the Hôtel de Ville and the Préfecture were burned down, and in one of these actions the Archbishop of Paris and the *curé* of Saint Sulpice were killed. On September 4 the Third Republic was declared.

On the day after the Commune Jules Simon had ordered obedience and tolerance, but, Mistral remarked, only God can command, and only the law of God can restore the people. It was about this time that he wrote to Albert de Quintana of the Catalan Academy these words: *Place au Christ et au Décalogue! Hors de lui et hors de là il n'y a que pourriture, sauvagerie et dissolution* ("Outside Christ and the Decalogue there is nothing but rottenness, savagery and dissolution"). At the beginning of September he wrote the poem *Roucas de Sisife* (*The Rock of Sisyphus*), touching the allegory of Sisyphus, whose pride would not allow him to free himself from his labor and submit to authority. The poem also concerned itself with the anticlericalism then mounting in France, and it expressed much the same sentiments as his letter to Quintana—outside Christ there was nothing but power, tyranny and chaos—recalling too the ancient law and making allusion to the priests massacred by the Communards. Some of the letters he wrote over this period strongly repudiated both the Communards and the *défense nationale* of Gambetta, and in one of them he cried indignantly that "we are the only people who deny our traditions, and are urged by our governments to impious hatred."

The fact is that Mistral's disillusionment with the revolutionary forces in France was complete. In 1870, refusing an official position (it was not the first or the last time that he had refused to stand as a candidate for the French Parliament), he had written, "Were I to participate in the work of a new Constitution, I would direct all my efforts to ensuring the success of the federal principle and I believe, alas, that this conception is not yet understood in France. Our French republicans dream of the advantages of the American and Swiss Constitutions but nearly all ignore or reject the only means of attaining them, which is federation."

Other events now helped to clarify his position. The restoration of the Spanish monarchy in 1870 had lasted but two years, and now the return of the republic brought anarchy in its wake. Mistral had to make a choice between liberty and authority, between the republic and the legitimate monarchy, between the fanaticism and chaos of the radicals on one hand and law and order, the divine right, on the other. In the autumn of 1872 he wrote to Quintana, "My soul is at peace." He had chosen.

While many Catalans were Carlists, that is Catholics and Monarchists, many were anticlerical, and this proved one of the dissonant factors in Mistral's alliance with such Catalans as Victor Balaguer and Albert de Quintana. Mistral, in fact, wrote in July, 1873 a poem in honor of Doña Blanca de Bourbon, sister-in-law of the Carlist pretender, which rather shocked his Catalan friends.

It was no use Mistral's trying to reassure them by saying that he wrote not as a politician but as a poet, for his sentiments were clearly expressed in his lines. 'Of silence I have had enough, and my heart burns with shame . . . Doña Blanca, holy woman, who goest forth to fight for God against the wicked world which prevaricates and blasphemes . . . Doña Blanca, defender of the Church which suffers . . . happy is he who falls at your feet.' To Quintana's protests Mistral replied expressing his sympathy for the Carlist cause and his intolerance of the democrats "who ruin, kill and make a laughing stock of the Latin world," while he pointed out the contrasting glory of "this young princess who mounts her horse and fights in the sun for the tradition of her race and for the religion of her ancestors." "I am logical in counselling you," Mistral ended, "not to forget that the old Catalans were Catholics and Monarchists."

The only flaw in Mistral's reasoning was the common error into which Léon Daudet, Charles Maurras and the *Action Française* were to fall. After 1870 the Republic became so hostile to the Church that Catholics tended to identify their religion with the Royalist party, and they had to be rebuked by Leo XIII in a significant document in which he reasserted the compatibility of Catholicism with any legitimate form of government, monarchical or democratic. More recently the corresponding mistake was made by the Sillonist movement, equally condemned for teaching that a good Catholic had to be republican.

During this period indeed Mistral might almost be regarded as a propagator of the Faith, and a French provincial newspaper[1] of some sixty years later has even referred to him as an 'apostle' in the light of two letters he wrote to his friend Alphonse Tavan in 1872-73. Tavan had been invalided out of the army with ma-

1. *La Pignato*, Toulon, 1933.

laria, and illness and poverty were now rendered even more unbearable by the death of his wife and, soon afterwards, of his only
child. He turned to his leader for comfort, and two noble letters
from Mistral deserve quoting in full:

Maillane, 26th November, 1872

My Poor Friend,
   I share fully the dreadful suffering which has cut you
to the heart. The mother was taken from you but left
the child to console you, and now the child in turn has
taken flight. Blessed are they that believe! Thanks be to
God, for them is left the hope that in the Kingdom of
Christ and the Virgin Mary they will see again in person those whom they loved. All other consolations are
useless, and I earnestly desire that religion will come to
help you in the immense grief which darkens your life.
Indeed this is the only happiness you can give the two
guardian angels who so prematurely were taken from
you. With all my heart as a man I grasp your hand.
                                              F. Mistral.

And the second letter a few months later:

Maillane, 11th March, 1873
   Yes, I understand and I feel deeply, my good friend
Tavan, that there is nothing in this world worse than to
lose those we love. The death of the person who loves
leaves less bitterness than the death of the beloved.
Happy are those who go first. Certainly I must seem to
be a happy man, and yet I say from the bottom of my
heart—happy are those who go first! I wish I could
soothe your wounds. But how to do it? I have heard that
you have lost the faith of your childhood . . . If that is
true, your misfortune is a dreadful one, for nothing on
earth can help a man whose horizon is bounded by the

grave. And if it were so, why should we grieve that
your two beloved ones have returned to the eternal
graveyard we call Nature? They feel nothing, they hear
nothing, and your grief is as vain as that of the madman
who would weep over dead leaves or the pebble lost in
the stream. If, on the contrary, you have kept that admirable Catholic Faith which explains everything and
makes everything bearable, I must tell you that you are
wrong to give way to despair. Those chaste, pure spirits
which blossomed with your transient love to give to you
a glimpse of a divine felicity are now in the world of
truth and light. They are like the cicada that has cast its
outer shell upon the earth and climbed into the tree to
sing. Why do you weep for them? They are not to be
pitied, they are free and immortal. That divine belief,
revealed by the words, by the miracles and by the death
of Christ, gives you a wonderful path towards them, by
prayer. Pray, for the God of our fathers has said that
prayer helps the poor dead. Pray and take courage, be
pure, be patient and resigned, if you hope one day to see
again the two companions who have left you. What can
you hope from the brutal materialism which covers the
mournful society of today with darkness? It can bring
you nothing but despair, agony, rage and misfortune.
The works of the greatest reformers, the republics of
Solon, of Lycurgus, of Plato and Brutus, fell into ruin as
completely as, and more quickly than, the empires of Tyrants. There is only one truth (which is distinctly shown
by history); it is that this world is a 'vale of tears', a
purgatory. And the greatest fools are those who, their
bodies subject to sickness, age and death, try to make
this world a paradise . . . You complain that you are
poor; a great poet, one of the greatest of this century,
Lord Byron, who possessed fame, fortune and beauty,
was seized before his thirtieth year with such a loathing

for the world and above all for humanity that he went to seek death in Greece . . . Become a Christian again, become a Catholic again and you will recover peace and hope. I am keeping your touching poems for the *Almanac*, and I trust that they will not be the last. It would give me great pleasure if you came to see me. Only, do warn me four or five days ahead, so that I don't make any other engagements that Sunday. Come, come, pull yourself together, remember that you are not a woman and that you need strength to continue to the end. I embrace you in friendship.

F. Mistral

These letters are filled with humanity and sincerity and the warmth of friendship. There is no religious cant, no claptrap about them. Yet Mistral's faith and belief shine through them, a faith quiet and unobtrusive yet steadfast, so different from the pessimistic Catholicism of a Lamartine or the aesthetic Catholicism of a Chateaubriand. It is difficult to suppose that a man who could write such things did not practice his religion in the orthodox manner, though, as Léon Tessier[2] has pointed out, in the Midi there are Catholics who keep Easter ceremonially and never enter a church for the rest of the year, and there are Catholics who go regularly to Mass but are reluctant to take the sacrament or even to enter the confessional. Mistral now wrote less religious poems and fewer pious notes in the *Armana*, and he seems to have bent the knee far less frequently than in his youth, yet the whole of his writing, his manner of speech and his daily life reflected an awareness of the presence of God and a profound theological knowledge. If he did not flaunt his faith in public places his influence for good, like that of the Carthusian in his cell, went out

2. *Mistral Chrétien* (Avignon, 1953), p. 64.

in subtle and unpredictable ways. More materially, he helped Tavan to find better employment doing a light job on the old Paris-Lyons-Marseilles railway.

The year 1872 had seen the publication of Daudet's play *L'Arlésienne*, though he had written it before the war. The theme, as indeed the title suggested, was Provençal, and it dealt with a similar frustrated love to that of *Mirèio*. Indeed it owed much, indirectly, to Mistral's friendship, for the basic story was inspired by incidents in and about Maillane, while the hero was given the name of Frederi. Originally *L'Arlésienne* appeared as a short story in the paper *Evénement* and then in *Lettres de mon Moulin*. It was constructed around two events that shocked and grieved Mistral's circle, first the suicide of Mistral's nephew at the ancestral Mas dou Juge, and then the tragic death of a youth at a farmhouse on the edge of Fontvielle. The setting of the play is La Castlelet, a simple *mas* white-walled in the sunlight, between Fontvielle and the reedy waters of the Vaccarès lagoon. Here the drama of frustrated passion is played out to emptiness.

Frederi loves a girl of Arles, a girl of unknown parentage and dubious social standing, whom his proud and prosperous parents are loath to accept though they reluctantly agree to the match. Then a *gardian* of the Camargue appears with letters to prove that he is the girl's cast-off lover. Frederi's code of honor compels him to renounce her for the sake of the family, and he agrees to marry Vivette, the virtuous and popular granddaughter of old Renaude, who genuinely loves him. But he is consumed by passion for the maid of Arles, and in his anguish he seeks the counsel of the patriarchal shepherd Balthazar, the old philosopher who watches the stars at night, who acts as intermediary between Frédéri and the Arlésienne. The betrothal of Frederi and Vivette takes place with feasting and the music of the farandole, but immediately after the festivities Frederi in the frenzy of despair takes his life by leaping out of a window into the courtyard. The plot is simple enough and the play is little more than a sequence of genre pictures, but the dramatic denouements, the sustained tension and the distracting and overbearing 'presence' of the maid of Arles—who, however, is never physically present and is never seen—all make for true drama.

The play was produced as an opera with music by Bizet in Paris the same year. It was a failure and its reception nearly broke Daudet's heart, though some thirteen years later it was to have a triumphant revival, as it deserved. The stage production has something of the hothouse atmosphere of D'Annunzio's *La Città Morta*, but Bizet's music, sympathetic and brilliantly evocative, is subservient to the play, and in the last act the music of the farandole rings out exultantly again and again before the final hush of tragedy. In the same year Daudet countered this stark presentation of Provence with another aspect of the *méridional* temperament in his *Tartarin de Tarascon*, but the buffoonery of the latter was not to the liking of the South—despite the native capacity for hyperbole and *galéjades*—and indeed parts of the Midi never forgave him for this caricature. Mistral was obviously not included in this hostile element; his affection for Daudet was too strong, and anyway his own sense of humor could appreciate Tartarin.

The smouldering passion of Daudet's *L'Arlésienne* and of other literary works dealing with the South was true enough to type, for the girls of Provence were noted for their ardor, and there was even a love language in flowers. Thus, as the Countess Martinengo-Cesaresco has reminded us, "Thyme accompanies a declaration; the violet means doubt or uneasiness; rosemary signifies complaint; nettle announces a quarrel."[3] The Countess goes on

3. *The Study of Folk Songs*, 1886.

to say: "As soon as a country girl is suspected of having a liking for some youth, she is set upon by her family as if she were guilty of a monstrous crime. A microscopic distinction of rank, a divergence in politics, or a deficiency of money will be snatched as the excuse for putting the lover under the ban of absolute proscription." It followed that a large number of Provençal marriages were the results of elopements (the period under review is that of Mistral's own lifetime), and that the hot-blooded maidens of the South sometimes sacrificed their virtue for love. Yet the women of Mistral's poems are all virtuous maidens—Mirèio, Nerto, L'Angloro and the young girl of the *Communion of Saints*, not forgetting Esterello, who though married was still *'libro et puro,'* free and a virgin. We have already noted the influence of John Stuart Mill on Mistral's ideal of womanhood, and it was in this year 1873 that Mill died in Avignon.

As we have seen, Mistral championed the cause of Carlism in Provence,[4] for the cause of Henri IV, supported by many people in the South, was virtually Carlist, and many of his friends shared his views, among them Scipion Doncieux and the Baron de Tourtoulon of Aix, one of the founders of the Paris branch of the Félibrige, a man who shared Mistral's dream of a Latin confederation and who, like Mistral, foresaw the rise of Germany and the threat of world war. This group of visionaries now attempted to expand the association with the Catalans until it included the whole Latin world. With the fifth centenary of the death of Petrarch in 1874 there came the opportunity to hold a festival in Avignon. Attended by a strong Italian deputation, this was a great success and led to another held with the Floral Games, organized by the Societé des langues romanes, in Montpellier in the following year. The latter occasion was memorable for a speech by Mistral which served once again to refute charges of separatism:

4. His claims to Carlism have been assessed by Camdessus in *Mistral était-il carliste?* (Bayonne, 1932)

... France, as you know, has not always hung her head over
her grieving heart; France, our mother, was once the queen
of nations in the arts of peace and in those of war. But, then,
people lived more naturally, and nobody was ashamed to
speak like his mother, and nobody blushed for his village
and, in order to love France it was not necessary to affect
French. For, whether one were called the Chevalier d'Assas
or the drummer of Arcola, when one had to go, one went;
when one had to die, one died.

... Do not let us forget, love of country is not the result of
opinion, or decree, or fashion. Great patriotism is born of
a man's attachment to his country, to his customs, to his family; and the best soldiers, believe me, are not those who sing
and who cry when they have drunk; they are those who
weep when they leave their homes.

Consequently, gentlemen, if we wish to restore our poor
country, let us restore that which breeds patriots: religion,
traditions, national memories, the old language of the country; and, city by city, province by province, let us compete
in study, work and honor, to exalt in different ways the name
of France. . . .[5]

The drummer of Arcola, referred to in the speech, was the subject of a ballad *Lou Tambour d'Arcolo*, an episode of the army in
Italy under Napoleon, which was included in a collection of Mistral's lyric poems published in this year of 1875. *Lis Isclo d'Or* or
The Isles of Gold contained the best of the shorter poems, the
songs, sonnets, elegies and religious pieces written over more than
a score of years. The title, said Mistral in the preface, may seem
ambitious "but I may be forgiven since one knows that it is the
name of a little group of arid rocky islands which the sun gilds
off the shore of Hyères. And may one not truly say that these
celestial moments of love, enthusiasm or sorrow are the oases, the

5. Quoted from Marius André, *La Vie Harmonieuse de Mistral*, in the translation of Rob Lyle, *Mistral* (Yale Univ. Press, 1953) p. 33.

isles of our existence?" This introduction was also largely auto-biographical, and though it was omitted from later editions it formed the core of Mistral's memoirs *Moun Espelido*. Thus the volume was filled with the life of Mistral and with the life of Provence, a brilliant cross-section of subject matter and of poetry construction in various forms.

It opens with a hymn to the sun *La Cansoun dóu Soulèu*, the life-giving sun of Provence, and the first section, *Li Cansoun*, the songs include *La Coupo*. There are episodes of Provençal history and legend, we meet *La Coumtesso* again, and there is a longer poem about *La Princesso Clemènco*, who was "as beautiful as the sea is vast." There is an elegy for Jasmine, the hairdresser-poet of Auch, there are the salutations to Lamartine, Gounod and others, there is the Ode to the Catalans and there are the Penitential Psalms. The religious pieces too are included here, among them the *Coumunioun di Sant* and *Lou Prègo-Diéu* (*The Praying Mantis*), the latter a melancholy meditation recalling the prayer to Our Lady of Montserrat, and rich in the paradox of life: "Flesh is lovely, and decays, the wave is bitter and I would drink. . . I want to die—and live . . . In the pleasures and in the pains of this world I also am bewildered, for as man grows he treads profanely. Love is God and love is sin . . .'"

A haunting poem on *Lou Blad de Luno* (*The Lunar Corn*) is followed by *Lou Lioun d'Arles* (*The Lion of Arles*), in which Mistral explores some local mythology and history. The lion-shaped peak above Saint Rémy in the Alpilles is locally supposed to be a petrified lion, presumably one of the lions associated with Arles, for the Municipality once kept these animals and the lion is still the emblem of the town. Mistral climbs to the peak to seek some mystic revelation: 'O ancient monster, immense and terrible sphinx, I come to thee in thy wisdom to seek the destiny of Provence . . .'

Here too are the Nuptial Songs, mostly written for such Félibres as Aubanel and Félix Gras, the Sonnets, and *Li Plang* or *The Laments*. This last section consists of somewhat enigmatic love poems, rivalling his friends Aubanel and Mathieu in amorous mood though they are marked by qualities of restraint and melancholy. They include a touching tribute to the dead young Félibresso Antonnieto de Beu-Caire, and they end with the elegy on the death of Lamartine.

The section of *Serventés* is divided from that of *Li Pantai* or *Dreams* by the superb and beautiful longer poem *La Fin dóu Meissounié* (*The Passing of the Reaper*), dated as early as 1853 and probably deriving from the unpublished poem called *The Harvests* written before Mistral was eighteen years of age. It catches a moment of human experience that is eternal, and it portrays the stoicism of human suffering. The old harvester lies mortally wounded in the cornfields, accidentally struck by the sickle of a young man behind him, for the old man moved slowly and the band of virile young men swept relentlessly on "like the wave of the sea." The others stood about grieving, women and children too. But the old harvester tells them not to weep but rather to rejoice, since he has ended his task before any of them. Life, like the reaping, must go on, and there is an allusion to the old ram who at last is killed by a young rival while the ewes, indifferent, go on cropping the grass. Never mind me, says the dying man, gather the ears of corn . . . the corn that comes from God. Then he remembers his family and his little olive garden, and with his arms raised and his eyes bright with mystery he calls on "Saint John of summer, lord Saint John, patron of reapers and father of the poor" to protect his wife and children, who "now, at Christmas, will eat without me." He asks forgiveness of his Maker and he dies. The reapers return in silence but in haste to their work, for the blazing sun which already boiled the blood in one's veins threatened to consume the corn in a mistral of flame.

The autumn of the year which followed the publication of *Lis Isclo d'Or* was notable for what was perhaps the happiest event in Mistral's life. It may seem remarkable that a virtuous, healthy, handsome man like Mistral should remain a bachelor until his forty-sixth year, and it is difficult to believe that he had no affairs of the heart in his youth (one does not forget the mysterious Louise, and here and there in his published work there are allusions to other women). The only explanation would seem to lie in his dedication to the Cause of Provence and poetry, and in his loyalty and devotion to his widowed mother, with whom he had now lived in the House of the Lizard for over twenty years.

It would seem that little or no courtship had preceded the marriage, for, wrote Mistral, "On the Tuesday after Whitsun I shall have my first interview with her who is to be my Esterello, if God so wills." Yet several of his letters make it clear that he was contemplating marriage well over two years earlier. Bonaparte-Wyse, in a letter dated January 1, 1874, after congratulating Mistral goes on, "I am not too sure that for an artistic nature like yours a marriage (even with an angel of the seventh heaven) would be a thing of good augury. . . Marriage is the tomb of the imagination. Family cares and ties are the enemies of the Muses."

Mistral said that his bride-to-be was "the child of an illustrious Provençal family, loyally Provençal by tradition and at heart." Mademoiselle Marie Rivière seems, however, to have had little Provençal background, for her father came from Vienne in Dauphiné and she had been brought up in Dijon. And it was in Dijon, in the Cathedral of Saint-Bénigne, that the marriage took place on September 27, 1876. Mistral was four years off fifty and his bride, his godchild, was barely twenty. Thus maturity and wisdom was wedded to youth in the second generation, just as his aging father had married the young Delaido. We would like to know more of Marie Rivière but there is little to record but the tributes of friends. Aubanel wrote that it was the marriage of "genius with beauty." Jean Ajalbert in later years referred to "her timid grace, her charming sweetness, her clear gaze and her fresh complexion," and "her sharp intelligence" . . . she was "the high priestess of the Mistral cult." Mistral himself wrote to Daudet, "I have found at last . . . the incarnation of that which I sought in Mirèio and Esterello." To another friend he wrote, "She is charming, beautiful, and is eager for great and heroic things."

Since the House of the Lizard was too simple and perhaps too small to accommodate three people, for of course his mother was not to be deserted, Mistral now built a new home immediately opposite the old one. It is a substantial but quite unimposing villa in the Second Empire manner and was officially described as "half town-house, half Provençal farm." It is set behind a high garden wall with iron spikes on the top of it, and its main assets for Mistral were undoubtedly the garden and the privacy. On the architraves of the front window Mistral had carved the star of Saint Estello, while the architraves of the rear windows were decorated with carved heads of Arlésiennes. Thus the Félibrige and the life of his Rhodanie dominated even his marriage.

CHAPTER 8

Nerto

THE STAR OF Saint Estello carved on the façade of Mistral's villa symbolized many things, and it was a reminder, if one were needed, of the annual Saint Estello banquet held in a different place each year. In 1878 it was held in Paris, where there was now a branch of the Félibrige, whose members frequented the Café Voltaire and the Café de Madrid. Since his marriage Mistral seems to have neglected his duties as an obedient son of the Church (despite the fact that he had a pious wife), and even his writings make less allusion to God and the Faith, though it was in this year that he began his translation of Genesis. In his speech at this Saint Estello banquet, however, he compared the work of the Félibres to the apostolic mission of the Apostles after they had received the gift of tongues at Pentecost:

> When our Redeemer descended from Heaven to earth the official, universal and indeed obligatory language was that of the Caesars. The language was as official as the slavery of the time. But Jesus, the Son of God, wishing his disciples to have in their hands the necessary means of freeing the people performed a miracle for them, which . . . approximates to our Félibrean Cause. At Pentecost the twelve fishermen were in a room where together they prayed to God. Suddenly the rushing of a mighty storm shook the house and languages

of fire lighted up the brows of the twelve apostles, while at the same time, filled with the Holy Ghost, they began to speak in different languages; and going out of the house they went into the midst of the multitude and they spoke to each man in his own language . . . and thus they went forth to rebuild the world.[1]

This may seem a purely Félibrean argument but nevertheless the words are those of an experienced and instructed Christian, despite the claims of the Félibrige to neutrality in the fields of religion and politics. Indeed these claims were now being asserted with more and more vehemence and consistency, so much so in fact that they were creating dissension within the Félibrige. Anti-clericalism was still making headway in France, but it was a year which saw the crowning of Pope Leo XIII, Gioacchino Pecci, *Lumen in Caelo* (The Light in the Heavens), "the Working Man's Pope," who made substantial repairs to the Church's deteriorating diplomatic relations with the world powers, insisted on the restoration of Thomist thought, and illumined Christian thinking on the rights of labor.

The Floral Games of 1875 held in Montpellier and the furtherance of hopes of a Latin federation led to an even greater concourse in the same university city in 1878. These games were organized by the Baron de Tourtoulon and lasted for seven days, with musical contests and shooting and the awarding of a silver cup, promoted by Quintana, for the best poem on the Latin race. It was an occasion of much pomp and ceremony, and Mistral's prestige was so high that he received the adulation of a national hero; as he drove in an open carriage from the station to the Peyrou the people sitting on the café *terrasses* stood up, the men raised their hats and cheered and the cafe orchestras played the

1. Léon Teissier, *op. cit.*, p. 70.

"*Coupo Santo.*" And Mistral must have remembered the awesome day, long ago, now, when he took his Baccalauréat under the hawk eyes of the yellow-gowned professors here. It was a gracious setting. Montpellier, with its celebrated school of medicine founded by Arab physicians driven out of Spain, was—and is—a beautiful town, its eighteenth-century Promenade de Peyrou set with classical pavilions and pools of blue water (the "antique garden" of Paul Valéry's *La Soirée avec Monsieur Teste*), and its elegant town houses sheltered behind secluded gardens of oak and laurel, among them the Hôtel Magnol which belonged to the botanist who gave his name to magnolias.

The prize was won by the Rumanian writer Vasile Alecsandri for his poem *La Gent Latine*. Alecsandri studied medicine, then law in Paris but abandoned both for literature; he made a study of popular ballads in Moldavia and became playwright and producer at the Iassy Roumanian Theatre. He was prominent in the political affairs of his native country—as early as 1859 he had played an active part in bringing about the union of the principalities—and the Montpellier award was no doubt partly a diplomatic gesture, though his poem had quality and fervor.

Mistral himself submitted a poem which he read out to the concourse on May 25, and this *Cant a la raço Latino*, a sublimation of his patriotic beliefs and aspirations, is undoubtedly superior to Alecsandri's poem:

> *Aubouro-te, raço latino,*
> *Souto la capo dóu soulèu!*
> *Lou rasin brun boui dins la tino*
> *Lou vin de Diéu gisclara lèu . . .*

> (*Arise, Latin people, beneath the cope of*
> *the sun! The dark grape foams in the vat,*
> *and the wine of God gushes forth.*

. . . . . .
Latin race in memory of your noble past
arise now with hope and fraternize
beneath the Cross.)

In the following year the Saint Estello feast was held in Toulouse, where Mistral spoke on the organization of the Félibrige. Toulouse was itself a great center of the *langue d'oc* and the home of the celebrated *Jeux Floreaux* or Floral Games, reputedly founded as early as 1323 by seven troubadours of the city, another instance of the mystic seven which may have influenced Mistral in his foundation of the Félibrige. The original object was to compete with poems on the Virgin for the prize of a golden violet (for Toulouse has always been a center of violets, fresh or candied). The Games were revived and Victor Hugo once carried off the prize. These were years filled with public appearances and speeches. In 1880 Mistral was speaking to another Félibrean concourse at Roquefavour:

When man, at twenty years of age, throws himself into the dense forest of life, to follow, to reach out and to grasp in his ardour one of those mirages which dance before his eyes down there—beauty, freedom, fame, conquest, what is it that intoxicates him, despite the gulfs which separate him from the realization of his ideal, what is it that consoles him, despite the misfortunes of those who fall, and what is it that spurs him on despite the discouragement of those who have experience of life? Gentlemen, it is Illusion.

Illusion, the balm of God, the shining mirror of youth, delight and mystery of love, and talisman of all happiness on our sad earth. Illusion, which impels the brave to acts of heroism, which makes the artist and the poet blossom, and excites them, and we might well believe if we were not Christian, that it is the symbol of virtue. . . Illusion, it is the dawn which, on the sharp and naked black summits of the mountain, casts each morning its mantle of white light with fringes of gold. Illusion is the fairy who lavishes, in the darkness, dreams of light.

It is not quite clear what Mistral meant by all this. Certainly some of his major poems, *Calendau*, *La Reino Jano* and *Lou Pouémo dóu Rose*, may be said to be works of illusion. *Calendau* as a story of chivalry and illusion has points of contact with *Don Quixote*, for in order to deserve the love of Esterello, Calendau must not only conquer his fellows by Herculean feats of prowess but he must also conquer himself. To be Calendau and yet not be Calendau. What Mistral was probably getting at, however, was the defence of his native land against the illusions of progress and political doctrinaires.

In 1882 a banquet was held at Montpellier in honor of Alecsandri and Bonaparte-Wyse, both doctrinaires imbued with the nebulous and indeed almost impossible idea of a Latin federation. The latter, who now lived in Avignon, in the Rue Pont-Trouca, where his second son Napoleon Estelle was born, had recently written a second book, *Li Piado de la Princesso* (*Footsteps of the Princess*), which was published in Avignon, Plymouth, Barcelona and Bucharest. The publication in Bucharest owed much to Bonaparte-Wyse's friendship with Alecsandri, to whom he dedicated the book, as Alecsandri later dedicated a book to Bonaparte-Wyse. The Rumanian patriot, like Mistral, was devoted to the restoration of his native tongue and the preservation of traditional life and costume, and he presented to Mistral's wife a choice specimen of Rumanian peasant costume.

It was about this time that Mistral's mother died. Delaido Poulinet, the mayor's daughter, had lived to see her son famous, and their devotion had been mutual and constant. Mistral, if he prac-

ticed what he preached in those letters to Tavan, was not likely
to mourn unduly, though his mother's passing must have been
a severe loss. There was now a wife to console him, and, besides,
his time was too fully occupied for grief to distract him for long.
Friends came to Maillane in an ever-increasing stream, and Daudet occasionally brought his son Léon to stay for a few days, when
with members of the Félibrige they would all set out for the day
to the Alpilles or Avignon or Arles. They would recite poetry and
sing old ballads of the Midi, but there were no longer the rollick-
ing escapades of former days. They were all mature aging men
now, with families and responsibilities. Arles was a favorite ob-
jective of Daudet, for a cousin named Montégut was a chemist
there and he had three sons to be companions for Léon. Then
there were visits to the Parrocels at Saint-Estève, a small estate
near Orgon beyond Saint Rémy. Monsieur Parrocel was descended from the family of well-known painters of that name, and he
and his wife were cultured and wealthy people who received such
distinguished guests from Paris as Edmond de Goncourt. Mistral
and his colleagues were often there, and Aubanel would be called
upon to recite his *Vénus d'Arles*, though unfortunately one would
no longer find Aubanel and Roumanille there at the same time.

Meanwhile an event had occurred which must have touched
Mistral sharply, though his reaction was an unorthodox one and
again showed his independence. This was the suppression in 1880
of the Prémonstratensian (or Norbertine) abbey of Frigolet, where
he had first gone to school, a governmental measure taken in the
political unrest of the period. The monks like those of other monasteries, refused to leave and the abbey was besieged by two thousand troops. The mayor of Maillane, Théophile Mistral, Mistral's
nephew, supplied the monks with provisions and other necessi-
ties, and some thousand peasants from the plain congregated
around the abbey in an attempt to drive away the soldiery, all to

no avail. The newspapers printed a confused story and made out that it was Mistral himself who had helped to defend the Fathers. Certainly Mistral attended the Mass celebrated on the last Sunday before the expulsion, for he said so in a letter to Ernest Daudet, adding "one is indignant with this interference with liberty . . . but it is not my affair." Not his affair; above all it was not the affair of the Félibrige! For Mistral refused to depart from the Félibrean principle of neutrality.

Just over twenty years later the Waldeck-Rousseau Laws of Association expelled all French Benedictines and Carthusians, and the pattern of resistance by the people was repeated. Nowhere was there more resistance than at the Grande Chartreuse, the venerable motherhouse of the Carthusian Order, in Dauphiné, where the government found it necessary to remove the twenty-three monks with a company of infantry, two squadrons of cavalry, a detachment of sappers and reinforcements of mounted police. The governmental charge of political intrigue was so palpably false that not a single lawyer in Grenoble could be induced to take up the legal defense of the government's action, and the mayors of thirty communes in the Dauphiné drafted a memorandum of protest, while many men of letters, notably François Coppée, voiced the indignation of his countrymen. Mistral seems to have been silent then also, and one is somewhat surprised and disappointed by the fact that he chose not to exercise his immense influence. It is another of the enigmas which surround him.

Yet in this same year as the siege of Frigolet the priests of Saint Sulpice in Paris, producing a crop of poems in all the languages of the world to celebrate the Immaculate Conception, commissioned Mistral to make the Provençal contribution. He accepted "because it is for the Holy Virgin" and because it would give pleasure to the Abbé Thomas, his childhood friend. The poem is essentially a litany of *méridionale* devotions to the Virgin. As poetry, with its touching invocation, it is splendid, but theologically we are on more uncertain ground. The majority of people then knew little about this new Catholic dogma, and they confounded the Immaculate Conception with the Virgin Birth. The Sulpician project was abandoned, however, but Mistral's poem was printed many years later in *Lis Oulivado* (when a stanza condemning materialism was omitted).

His next major work appeared in 1884. *Nerto* is a departure from *Mirèio* and *Calendau* both in context and poetic form; it has no political or meridional axe to grind, and the construction has changed from Mistral's normal sequence of stanzas to rhymed octosyllabic couplets. It is frankly a fairy story based on Provençal legend and its setting is Avignon, Arles and the Alpilles early in the fifteenth century. The heroine derives her name, Nerto, from the Provençal name for the myrtle, of which there were many in Mistral's garden. Nerto's soul has been vowed to the Devil by her father, and though this melodramatic, operatic and Faustian theme did not appeal to Gounod an opera was in fact written for it by Widor.

Nerto learns upon her father's death that he had sold her soul to the Devil, and she journeys to Avignon to implore the aid of the Pope, Benedict XIII. Here Mistral weaves into the narrative a history of the events at Avignon brought about by the Great Schism, when Christendom was divided by two rival Popes, one in Rome and the other here in Avignon. It is difficult to grasp just what this meant to medieval society, when, technically, everyone was excommunicated and the nations of Europe were ranged on opposing sides. England, Germany and Italy supported the Rome claimant, while France, Spain, Portugal and Scotland were on the side of the Avignon Pope. The Low Countries made some half-hearted attempt at neutrality, resulting in some curious anomalies. In Bruges, for instance, the Carthusian monks held for

Avignon, while the Carthusian nuns there held for Rome. Avignon was thus a city unique in its power and influence and consequently unique in its character and atmosphere. Heretics found asylum there. Jews obtained toleration by the payment of a small tax. The streets were thronged with cardinals, penitents, ambassadors, scholars, jongleurs, soldiers and seamen, and if it was a city of piety it was also a city where pleasure was confounded with vice.

Nerto arrives at the Papal Palace during the historic siege, and there she meets Roudrigo, the Pope's nephew, who falls in love with her. Nerto obtains an audience of the Pope, but the tumult has intensified and the great palace is now on fire. Pope Benedict appears to the people and bestows the papal blessing, *urbi et orbi*, and the last Pope to reign in Avignon, a tragic figure, disappears "like the sun at twilight" to escape to the royal castle of Châteaurenard (Mistral, following the legend, contrives the escape by an underground passage, though in fact the Pope escaped by boat). These episodes are brilliantly portrayed, and there is a splendid evocation of the Avignon of the time.

Louis, King of Anjou and Count of Provence, arrives with his suite at the castle to seek the papal blessing upon his marriage, and the marriage in Saint Trophime in Arles, together with the celebrations and the fights in the arena, is described. Meanwhile, on the Pope's advice, Nerto enters a convent and takes the veil in the presence of Pope, King and Queen. It seems that Nerto has followed the Pope's advice against her own heart, and now she mourns the monastic sacrifice of her beautiful hair. Despite the fact that she is virtually the Pope's protégée, Roudrigo breaks into the convent by night and abducts her, not entirely against her will though naturally she has qualms. Roudrigo is attacked during the process and is forced to abandon her somewhere in the Alpilles. Nerto now flees to a holy hermit. Despite the hermit's sanctity, however, he appears to be somewhat human and persuades her to live with him in order, so he says, that they may pray together. The situation is delicate, but the hermit may genuinely be a holy man momentarily stricken by a "Temptation of Saint Anthony." Fortunately an angel appears to rescue Nerto from this dilemma and to compel the old man to send her back to the convent.

Roudrigo in his carnal passion, however, seems to have persuaded the Devil to create an enchanted castle to which Nerto is lured. Then the Devil, Nerto and Roudrigo all meet, and Roudrigo, softened by the maiden's beauty repents, and when Satan claims his due Roudrigo, inverting his sword and holding up the pommelled cross, cries "In the name of the Father, Son and Holy Ghost, get thee behind me." The castle disappears in a sheet of flame and a roll of thunder, leaving nothing but a rock shaped like a kneeling nun. In an epilogue Nerto and Roudrigo enter Paradise.

Despite what may be called the triteness of the story, it is filled with Christian philosophy and has marked qualities of asceticism, and it is the most strikingly religious of Mistral's works. In a letter to Félix Hémon, dated January 14, 1886, Mistral reveals his intentions:

Here is the philosophical or rather the theological idea of the book. A son of Catholicism, I have felt often a great sadness in seeing the inconsistency between religious belief and modern ideas. The march of progress seems to defy and humiliate the old traditions of Christian renunciation, and as I wish to be of my century without denying my faith, as I do not believe that one century can be always right and another always wrong, and as I see in the development of humanity an harmonious progression, here is the explanation which I have chosen for myself and which I have indicated in Nerto in some very laconic verses: Progress is a manifestation from God, a sequel to his eternal creation; but if God is the Architect the Devil is the labourer, and the punishment of the Devil and of diabolic pride lies in seeing his work turned finally to the glory of God.

A veneration for sanctity was unquestionably a hallmark of Mistral's life and work, and one feels that here at least he held common ground with Victor Hugo. "Is there in this world a glory greater than that of the poet?" a flatterer once asked Hugo. "Yes, that of the saint," replied the author of the *Contemplations*. In *Nerto*, in fact, Mistral returns to the Christian ideal of *Mirèio*. More, in this poem he is not content merely to be a Christian but becomes a theologian, and the prelude dealing with demonology shows a remarkable conception of the Devil and his works (though some might hold that it is folklore again), as indeed the entire poem shows a remarkable knowledge of Catholic doctrine. His brilliant championing of the Avignon Popes leaves no doubt as to which side he was on. Not unexpectedly, *Nerto* was awarded the Prix Vitet and was virtually the occasion of a much later papal blessing. Many more honors would easily have come his way, but he was choosy, or at least wary, and he did not wish to lose his identity as one of the common people. "*Nous avons fait route avec les pauvres. C'est avec eux qu'il faut rester.*" (We have always gone along with the poor. We must stay with them.) Thus, about this time, he declined membership of the French Academy. In this year too he resigned as Capoulié or leader of the Félibrige in favor of Roumanille. He had after all held the fort for thirty years and he felt that he could dominate it no longer, though he remained the presiding spirit and even constitutional monarch.

The year following the appearance of *Nerto*, 1885, was crowned with another success of a quite different order. Over a score of years had gone to the writing and production of *Lou Tresor dóu Felibrige*, a work of great erudition and perseverance which places Mistral among the masters of philology, as his occasional gleanings published in the *Armana* and the footnotes to his major poems place him among the leading anthropologists. At the head of this Provençal dictionary-encyclopaedia he inscribed the sonnet *Au Miejour* (*To the Midi*):

> In working and faring badly for the name of Provence I have created what is provided here, and, God having helped me to accomplish my task, kneeling in the furrow, I give thanks today to God. O people of the Midi listen to my words. If you would reconquer the empire of your language, to be clothed anew, draw from this treasury.

He had begun work on the *Tresor* at the beginning of 1862. Language, as we have seen, was of the utmost importance to Mistral, and he regarded it indeed as the "master-root of all patriotism, the powerful leaven of all freedom." His speech at the Saint Estello banquet of 1877 reveals his veneration for the mother tongue:

> A language is like the shaft of a mine for at the bottom of it there have been deposited all the fears, all the feelings, all the thoughts, of ten, twenty, thirty, a hundred generations. It is a pile, an ancient hoard, whither every passer-by has brought his gold or silver or leather coin. It is a great monument whither every family has carried its stone, where every city has built its column, where a whole race has worked, body and soul, for hundreds and thousands of years. A language, in a word, is the revelation of actual life, the manifestation of human thought, the all-holy instrument of civilizations, and the speaking testament of dead and living societies.[2]

2. Quoted in the translation of C. M. Girdlestone, *Dreamer and Striver* (Methuen, 1937).

This dictionary, then, was more than a dictionary, for it was a lexicon and an encyclopaedia to Provençal history, folklore, traditions, customs, trades and occupations, furniture, costume, trees, flowers and herbs and almost everything else, delving into Greek, Latin, Hebrew and other languages, and illustrated whenever possible by the proverbs and sayings of the people. It was the product of laborious research and of numerous conversations with savants and peasants, with fishermen and agricultural laborers. The manuscript alone ran to 14,000 pages, and the final work in two volumes contained 2,400 closely printed pages. The first draft was completed in 1874, but proofreading, arguments with critics, publishers and subscribers and the actual printing and binding, by the Séguin brothers of Avignon, delayed publication. According to Mistral's own accounts he received 44,427 gold francs for the work, but his costs amount to just over 3,000 gold francs more. Fortunately in 1890 he was awarded the Prix Jean Reynaud, worth 10,000 gold francs, by the Académie des Inscriptions et Belle lettres, one of the constituent bodies of the Institut de France. Yet to Mistral monetary considerations were not of primary importance (he had been left comfortably off by his father and had never been compelled to write for money), and this immense labor of love earned the plaudits of the savants and the gratitude of his countrymen. It was, to quote his friend Bruno Durand, keeper of the library at Aix, a "Triple mystery of love, of patriotism, and of genius.'

Daudet came again to Maillane, bringing with him young Léon and the highly neurotic and artistic Edmond de Goncourt, who with his brother Jules (who died in 1870) had begun the celebrated *Journal des Goncourt*, was the author of novels dealing with abnormal types, and was an authority on Japanese art. Mistral and Daudet spent some time in the Camargue at the Mas de Vers, where they mingled with the *gardians* and explored, to

Léon's delight, the reedy islets of the Vaccarès lagoon. The episode, reinforced by his memories of a winter there long ago, was to provide the material for Daudet's grim story of the Camargue, *Le Trésor d'Arlatan*, a tale of a fevered mind, of corruption and suicide. This was the year in which Daudet's *L'Arlésienne* was revived in Paris and was a great triumph, though Bizet had not lived to see it, having died ten years earlier on the twenty-third day of his opera *Carmen*. The controversy with Paul Arène had not yet broken, and Arène was himself to have a success in the following year with his novel *La Chèvre d'Or*.

The year 1885 also saw the appearance of Aubanel's *Li Fiho d'Avignoun*. A few years earlier, in 1878, his savage and distracting play *Lou Pan dòu Pecat* (*The Bread of Sin*) had been produced in Provençal at Montpellier, and later a French translation by Arène was successfully mounted at the Odéon in Paris, though Aubanel did not live to see the realization of a dream which he had often discussed with Bonaparte-Wyse and Daudet. An earlier play *Lou Pastre* (*The Shepherd*), based on a sordid case of rape at Carpentras, was unsuccessful. The latest work, published in French as *Les Filles d'Avignon* (*The Girls of Avignon*), was a book of erotic poems inspired by Avignon's infamous *quartier reservé* (the prostitutes' quarter which also inspired a well known painting by Picasso). Aubanel was perhaps the only member of the group capable of seeking and expressing absolutes in the manner of Verlaine. An ardent practicing Catholic, he was yet a man of passion, combining Christian feeling with pagan sensuality; perhaps the affair with his 'Zani' had obsessed him with a sense of the tragedy of life and had checked his spiritual expansion. *The Girls of Avignon* sang frankly of the flesh, and Aubanel's enemy Roumanille denounced it in no uncertain terms to the Archbishop of Avignon. The book, like his *La Miougrano entreduberto*, was censored and placed on the *Index*. This may have hastened Aubanel's end, for he died in the following year, on the last day of October, 1886. This was a sad occasion for Mistral, who had only recently made a speech eulogizing his friend on Aubanel's entry into the Marseilles Academy. Aubanel was buried in the habit of a Pénitent Blanc in Avignon, and over the grave on All Saints Day Mistral spoke these words: "Confessor of God throughout your life, today in the bosom of God, you now embrace forever the supreme beauty of your dreams, that beauty which you revealed to us in your burning poetry."

With his numerous public engagements and speeches, his voluminous correspondence and the business of the Félibrige it is remarkable that Mistral undertook as much literary work as he did. With *Nerto* and the *Tresor* now safely launched, he was already researching for yet two more long poems. He rose at seven after a light breakfast of *café au lait* with perhaps a roll, which he seems to have taken in bed or at least in his bedroom. He worked in his study until noon, mainly writing letters and attending to an enormous incoming mail, while there was always the newspaper *l'Argus de la Presse*, which dutifully reported all Félibrean activities. He lunched rather frugally on peasant regional dishes, taking little meat and drinking only a little wine from his own vine mixed with water, nor did he take coffee at that time of day. If he had guests then, of course, Madame Mistral and the servant Marie-du-Poète concocted more ambitious dishes, and a choice Provençal wine, Tavel or Châteauneuf-du-Pape, came up from the cellar. During the afternoon he read and received a continuous flow of guests, and before dinner he walked, often with his wife, at least four or five kilometers. Edmond de Goncourt, describing a meeting with the poet at Daudet's home at Champrosay in 1884, records that Mistral made it clear that he worked best in the twilight hours and that in the morning the fields about Maillane were too full of clamor to do concentrated work. He dined at seven and usually retired to bed about nine o'clock, which seems somewhat early. Very rarely now did he venture in the evening to the Café dou Soulèu, there to take coffee and smoke a cigar.

The garden claimed much of his time, a garden of peace and magic behind a wall crowned with a hedge of laurels, rich in myrtles, roses that bloomed for six months of the year, sunflowers, red violets, petunias, Queen Marguerites, and *ancolies* (a kind of ranunculus), an abundance of flowers and beds of verbena and balsams all fragrant in the hot sun. It was the garden of a romantic, "the garden of a priest or of a poet" a friend called it, as another friend referred to the house as a hermitage. There too was the vine and the fig tree, the well and the seat turned toward the front door with its smiling head of an Arlésienne.

Madame Mistral and Marie (who was a devoted and privileged domestic) had their work cut out in protecting him from the many unwelcome callers and busybodies as well as ushering in and attending to more welcome guests, and these now included a high proportion of celebrities. These guests would find themselves in an entrance hall filled with paintings, photographs, statues and medals concerning Mistral's works, especially *Mirèio*, and these overflowed into the study where there were also maquettes of the poets and busts of Gounod and Lamartine by Jean Baptiste Carpeaux, the leading sculptor of the Second Empire, whose group *Dancing* is to be seen on the Paris Opéra. On the other side of the hall was the drawing room with couches and chairs lacquered in sea green. Elsewhere there was a good deal of mahogany furniture, and wallpapers seem mostly to have been flowered in brown and beige. Walls were hung with trophies, copper ornaments, Moustiers porcelain and enamelled green jugs from Sisteron, while there was a special place of honor for the gun which Mistral *père* had carried with the Grande Armée. The hall also led into the white dining room, which Paul Aréne compared to the interior of a lighthouse, where at Christmas Madame Mistral would set up and dress the traditional crib.

CHAPTER 9

The Cult of Mithra

IN ARLES there was now talk of a mad red-haired Dutch painter who lived in a small yellow house on the Place Lamartine, where he had moved from a room above the Restaurant Carrel, the *Night Café* of his celebrated picture. The painter's name was Vincent Van Gogh. It was the autumn of 1888. We see something of Arles at this time through Van Gogh's letters—"the Zouaves, the brothels, the adorable little Arlésiennes going to their first communion, the priest in his surplice, who looks like a dangerous rhinoceros, the people drinking absinthe. . ." There was Roulin, the kindly postman who often sat for him; there was the amorous Milliet, the lieutenant of the Zouave regiment, a stocky fellow with a neck like an ox and flaming eyes; there was Madame Giroux, the subject of his portrait *L'Arlésienne*; there was Madame Chose and her accommodating if naughty girls, including the wild Nanette, the little brunette from Avignon who pulled his ears; and there were his friends of the Café Giroux where he drank absinthe in the afternoon.

Van Gogh painted the porch of Saint Trophime, which was "cruel and monstrous . . . like a Chinese nightmare," the local park blossoming with oleander and lustrous with cedar and cypress, the Alyscamps, the drawbridge on the edge of the town with the yellow cart and the washerwoman by the stream, the gypsy camp at Les Saintes-Maries, the giant sunflowers, the olive harvests, the orchards with their ephemeral peach and pear tree blossoms and the silvery trees against the red ochre soil. The country about Arles "seems to me as beautiful as Japan for clarity of atmosphere and gay colour effects. Water forms patches of lovely emerald or rich blue in the landscape, just as we see it in the crape-prints. The pale orange of the sunsets makes the fields appear blue. The sun is a splendid yellow."[1] This was indeed the Empire of the Sun. And thus Van Gogh recorded and interpreted 'Rhodanie' as Mistral had sung it in verse. But here was the third dimension—it was as different from the Provence of Mistral as it was from that of Daudet. Here was the element of savagery, undisciplined, a sensuous surrender to a strange, colorful and sometimes violent world.

Mistral must certainly have heard about him. Did he meet him? There was no reason why he should; the two had nothing in common. Yet Mistral with all his humanity may have been concerned when a little later Van Gogh, sick in mind and body, began his downward path. For since Van Gogh had cut off his ear and sent it to Nanette he was now openly jeered at by the townspeople, who gathered outside his house and shouted "*Fou-roux! Fou-roux!*" The little yellow house became famous—or infamous —as *la maison du fou*. Soon he had to go into the local hospital. Further disorders followed on his discharge, and nearly a hundred citizens clamored for his removal to an asylum. The Protestant Pastor Salles did what he could, but Monsieur Pardieu, the Mayor of Arles, had to order the painter's incarceration.

Presently he was removed to the asylum of Saint Paul du Mausolée, the old convent which Mistral had taken Gounod to see, on

1. *Letters to Emil Bernard*, Ed. Douglas Lord (London, 1938).

148

the edge of Saint Rémy and within easy walking distance of Mail-lane. Here, under the direction of Dr. Peyron, Van Gogh was nursed by the sisters of Saint Joseph d'Aubenas (who had now replaced the sisters of Saint Vincent de Paul). From the iron-grilled window of his small room he would gaze upon the golden cornfields and the wide blue Provençal sky, islanded in the long silences broken only by occasional sobbing or hollow laughter. He read Shakespeare and he painted, sometimes in the compara-tive freedom of the cloister gardens. Among his canvases was that of the reaper in the corn, a subject which he portrayed as brilliantly, framing a moment of time, as Mistral in his *La Fin dóu Meissounié*. On May 17, 1890, he left for his brother's home in Paris, and a warder accompanied him as far as Tarascon. It was a strange interlude in the life of Arles.

Like Daudet, and like Aubanel, Mistral had long hoped to write a drama, and his work in this field came to fruition with the publication in 1890 of *La Rèino Jano* (Queen Joan). It met with only a limited success, however, and since it was never performed on the stage it may be regarded as a failure. National dramas are not the most popular of stage plays, and *La Rèino Jano* is of this genre, a tragedy in five acts dealing with episodes in the life of Joanna, Queen of Naples and Countess of Provence, crowned in 1343, who is tried and acquitted on a charge of murdering her husband Andreas, brother to the King of Hungary. Mistral in his introduction to this drama made the following observation: "Queen Joan belongs to that group of historic figures—Caius Mar-ius, Ossian, King Arthur, the Count Raymond of Toulouse, our good King René, Anne of Brittany, Roland, the Cid and others—with whom popular tradition associates heroic legends, national pride and mysterious public buildings." Among these 'mysterious public buildings' (*monuments mystérieux*) is that still pointed out in Avignon as "the House of Queen Joan," and in his introduction Mistral lists all the châteaux of Provence which belonged to her, "while all the Renaissance palaces in Avignon, Villeneuve, Toulon, Draguignan, Lorgues and Saint Rémy were built and inhabited by her."

The first three acts of the play are laid in fourteenth-century Naples, but the first is filled with allegory and praise of Provence. In the third act the assassination of the King has less plausibility than a 'cloak and dagger' murder of our own time. The fourth act is largely taken up with the voyage from Naples to Provence over the enchanted sea ("the sea is an enchantress") and the triumphant reception of the Queen, which is a departure from historical fact. The final act deals with her trial for murder and her acquittal (though the real Joan was finally captured in Naples and murdered by the Duke of Durazzo), and this is an act so filled with choruses that it becomes grand opera.

Mistral was not merely a storyteller and a savant; he was an observer of life, and *La Rèino Jano*, like *Nerto*, is an historical pageant. Yet when it suits his purpose he plays rather freely with history, and it must be admitted that much given as fact is highly questionable. Despite popular tradition, Queen Joan spent only six months in Provence and exploited the country for her own ends. Again, it was quite impossible for her to have built the church of Santa Chiara in Naples, which was completed a score of years before she was born. Mistral being Mistral could do no other than eulogize that Joan who 'for the people of Provence . . . dominates like a good fairy the history of the country in the time of its independence.' It is certain that some of the people had long confused her with that Joan who was the wife of 'good King René.' Was the real Joan the ascetic abbess-like figure whose portrait by an anonymous painter is to be seen in the Musée de Versailles? Was not Mistral's Joan an incarnation of Provence, utterly opposed to the powerful, cruel and amorous Queen of Naples who had sold Avignon to Pope Clement VI and had commandeered the wealth and flower of Provence for the reconquest of Naples? No matter, Mistral had created a heroine who represented the most highly developed type of womanhood, combining passion and feminine intuition with competence, intelligence and courage; she was the Countess, she was Doña Blanca. In her crusade for freedom and the good of the people she was also another Elizabeth of Hungary, even another Joan of Arc. And she was, inevitably, the symbol of Mistral's ideal pattern of government.

Having written about Naples Mistral visited it in the spring of the following year, making the journey with his wife. This Italian tour was an occasion which offered the utmost opportunity to affirm his faith, but the fact is that he seems to have made little of it. He spent eight days in Rome but made no attempt to seek an audience of the Pope. In Naples he went to Mass at the church of Santa Chiara, a Baroque confection with its cloister of nuns, its walls and benches of majolica and its trellised vines.[2] On the afternoon of the same day he went to the cathedral of San Gennaro just in time for the celebrated annual miracle of the liquefaction of the blood of the patron saint—"the priest displayed the liquified blood, which bubbled up, purple, in two little ampules. One after the other, in crowds, the men kissed it devotedly, as one kisses the holy arm at Les Sainte Maries. Saint Januarius is here the symbol of local patriotism, and even the sceptics do not speak of him without respect." Mistral met a number of celebrities, including Carducci, then professor of rhetoric at the university of Bologna. It is difficult to believe that the two had much in common, for Carducci was a free thinker and an anti-Christian for most of his life, though his later work showed some softening in his attitude. Nor could Mistral have agreed with Carducci's view

2. This largely disappeared in the bombing of 1943.

that the age of epic poetry was past, though they could compromise on the latter's agreement that some episodes of history could be more efficiently communicated in verse than prose. Altogether Mistral was well received in Italy; even a Customs officer waved the baggage aside and saluted when shown the diploma certifying Mistral an Officer of the Corona d'Italia (awarded at the Petrarch celebrations in Avignon). The tour was, however, overshadowed by one event, the death of Roumanille, of which news reached Mistral in Venice.

Joseph Roumanille died thirty years after he had written, "Now, Lord, I can die, now that I have seen the tree which I planted in Provence flourish." The father of the Félibres died full of faith and virtue, and on his deathbed he may have thought of Aubanel. In his last moments he raised his hand and held it there, waveringly. "What are you seeking?" asked his wife. "I am seeking the hands of friends that I may grasp them." And so he died. The tree he planted, the Félibrige, still flourishes, and on the Rue Saint-Agricol in Avignon there stands the Librairie Roumanille which he also founded. On the Square Saint Martial of that town a memorial was inaugurated by Mistral in 1904. It is a plinth carved with a garland of symbolic flowers and, in relief, a bronze depicting the two heroines of Roumanille's poem *Li Sounjarello*. But it was to his native soil at Saint Rémy that Roumanille's body was returned, and there, outside the Hôtel Dieu, is his monument; he is seated, holding a book in one hand and his eyeglass in the other, and though the sculptor has not made enough of the ample locks and beard there is something bardic, almost Shakespearian, about the figure.

In this same year, 1891, Roumanille's daughter Térèse, who was a Queen of the Félibrige, married Jules Boissière, the poet of *Opium Fumes* and *Bhudda*. They went out to Hanoi, and when they returned they filled their house with Indo-Chinese furniture and *objets d'art;* like other interiors of the period the house was as rich and heavy as plum cake. Mistral and Bonaparte-Wyse were frequent visitors there, drinking tea from Annam and *thé de mandarin,* brewed from dried up flowers fresh from the lotus or the jasmine, which Térèse knew how to prepare.

Meanwhile Mistral had launched his Provençal paper or journal *L'Aioli,* founded with the money of the Prix Jean Reynaud. It may be thought that in the annual *Armana Prouvençau* he had an adequate vehicle for his crusade, but other considerations now made him feel that he should be in closer touch with the Provençal masses in a medium which left no doubt as to his opinions and policy. In addition to the State's insistence on French in the schools and its attitude to regional tongues, there were growing dissensions within the Félibrige itself, and the Paris members in particular were creating trouble with their factions and cliques. As early as June, 1889 Mistral seems to have had the idea of this new organ in mind, when he went to Paris for discussion, and it was probably at dinner in the home of the Duc d'Aumale that he first planned the paper, as he may then have decided to appoint as assistant editor the young Folco de Baroncelli, one of his faithful followers, whose parents were at the dinner party. The title of the paper, *L'Aiòli,* was a happy one, since it was simply the name of the popular Provençal sauce compounded of mayonnaise and garlic and would appeal to the peasant class. Such an inspiration was not without precedent, however, for there had been an earlier Tarascon paper called *La Bouillabaisse,* after the fish stew of the South.

The first number of *L'Aiòli* appeared on January 7, 1891, and it was designed to appear three times a month, on the 7th, 17th and 27th, in accordance with Mistral's 'Nostradamus' whim. The front page bore an illustration of a group of peasants outside a *mas,* with one man holding a mortar and mixing up the mayonnaise with a pestle as a young woman poured in the olive oil, while in the background there was a panorama of Avignon. In his open manifesto Mistral made it clear that the *aiòli* was a symbol and that in the making of it they would "stir up and fortify Provençal matters in our own language." *L'Aiòli* in its essence "concentrated the heat, the strength, the gaiety of the sun of Provence. . ." And he goes on to make his mayonnaise symbolic of the union of the provinces of the Midi, denouncing the "northern frost," the "*Franchiman's* arrogance" and asserting once more his claims for federation. Among the earliest contributions to the paper were tributes to Roumanille and Mistral's letters from Italy (later published in a French translation by Charles Maurras).

The need for such a medium as *L'Aiòli* was in fact soon proved, for the conflict between the Félibres came to a head in the following year at a banquet in Paris given in honor of Félix Gras, Roumanille's brother-in-law and an anticlerical, who had succeeded Roumanille as *Capoulié*. On this occasion a manifesto written by Charles Maurras and Frédéric Amouretti was read out. It was undoubtedly a 'Carlist' declaration but it really did little more than reaffirm the Mistralian concept of federation, calling for freedom for "Gascons, Auvergnats, Limousins, Béarnais, Dauphinois, Roussilonnais, Provençaux and Languedociens." It was, however, more than the factious element could bear, and the Jacobins in particular attacked it. Mistral, who was not present at the banquet, printed the manifesto on the front page of *L'Aiòli* with his own endorsement, which seems to have widened the rift in Paris for Maurras and Amouretti were expelled from the Paris Félibrige. These two ardent Mistralians (later to cause the Master such embarrassment) then gathered another group about them, so that it would appear that there were virtually *two* Paris branches of the Félibrige, though the new shoot must have lacked 'official' recognition and status. Nor was this the last of such troubles.

As the organization developed such differences were perhaps inevitable, though much of the unrest may be attributed to Mistral's resignation as *Capoulié* and to the loss of Roumanille's steadying influence.

William Bonaparte-Wyse, then living in his Irish manor of Saint John in County Waterford, was spared much of this trouble and anxiety, and it was now that he made his last journey to Provence. He knew instinctively that it was the last, for he wrote to Mistral saying that he had come to die "amid the sunshine and the flowers." He wished to lie near the hills of the fairy Estello, where the blue butterflies—his *papillons bleus*—would come to dart about his grave and the Provençal sun would warm his tombstone. And so it was. On December 3, 1892, he died at Cannes while at work on a translation into Provençal of his poem *Bacchus in Provence*, which was already appearing in serial form in *L'Aiòli*. A year or so earlier he had been feted at Montpellier, where the menu had contained dishes named after his principal poems. Mistral had never made that journey to England after all, but only recently he had written to Bonaparte-Wyse expressing a wish to cross the Channel. The Irishman had replied promising Mistral a splendid reception in London by the poets and writers—"and if you would extend your journey to Ireland you would find me like the cicerone in the *Inferno*, with the difference that it would be I who would guide Virgil through the circles. . . I would show you that I have not forgotten those days at Châteauneuf. . . Have you heard of the lakes of Killarney? There is nothing in the world more ravishing, more filled with a fairylike beauty. Come there with me." But now it was too late. Bonaparte-Wyse was dead.

The achievement of William Bonaparte-Wyse was really quite unique. The mastering of the Provençal language and the dexterity with which he wrote Provençal poetry was remarkable enough, but even more than this was the man's vision, the pursuit of an ideal and his devotion to and unstinted effort for the Félibrige. He had at first regarded the movement as a kind of swan song, a despairing revolt against the domination of the *Franchiman*, a mere eddy like the backwash which rushes against the main current of the Rhône. Then it became a Cause, the eddy was itself to become the main stream. He did not believe in a lingua franca which the entire world would speak. Every nation should have its own language. As he said at Forcalquier in 1882, "The native speech of a country is a bond which binds the people to the soil, and it should be regarded with a favourable eye by every statesman who thinks for the future." He was the first stranger deliberately to make his own the heritage of Provence, and as the ambassador of the Félibrige he carried the standard to Britain, to Spain, to Italy, to Rumania. Without his unflagging zeal and idealism the movement may well have remained in obscurity outside France. What may seem surprising, however, is that he did not devote all this energy and single-mindedness of purpose to Irish affairs, to the Gaelic Revival taking root in his own soil during his lifetime.

Mistral's oldest friends were going quickly now. In the following year Gounod and Paul Arène died. In the next year, 1894, Brunet went, and in the year after that his old schoolfriend Anselme Mathieu. Gounod, reconciled to France after the war, died at Saint Cloud. Arène died at Antibes but was buried in his native Sisteron. Brunet died so poor that he was buried at the expense of his native town, Avignon, leaving no poetry of value but an important work containing 14,000 Provençal proverbs. And Mathieu, who had made little out of either writing or hotel keeping, was buried in his native Châteauneuf-du-Pape. Apart from poor old Tavan, Mistral was now the only survivor of the original Félibrige (Paul Giéra, the first to go, had died as early as 1861). In the fullness of his years he now resembled one of the patriarchs in his own epics. Jean Ajalbert, describing him in 1894, observed that:

> He has changed without aging. At sixty-four, age, in some extraordinary way, has not touched him. Upright, strong, very handsome, the eyes of youth set in a wide and smiling face with moustaches and Imperial beard, the high broad brow crowned with vigorous hair almost tonsured by the years at the top and at the back. What there is of the theatrical, of the musketeer in the form of the *Capoulié*, is attenuated. He is, as De Goncourt has also noted, like a handsome and solid peasant who has abandoned the smock. In Paris I had found him a little provincial (strictly *méridional* or of the south), but here Mistral is natural, in keeping with his countryside, and with his genius, simple, intimate and grand.[3]

A little earlier, in the spring of 1892, Madame Darmesteter, English wife of the French orientalist and philologist, "went more than once to see the great man in his garden at Maillane, a pleasant place surrounding a cool quiet villa, where the poet lives with his young wife. It is the only house of any pretensions in Maillane, and to the good people of the commune Monsieur Mistral is both the poet and the squire. He comes out to receive you—a strikingly handsome man with a beautiful voice . . . much like Buffalo Bill in his appearance."[4]

Mistral, however, was now much more than the 'squire' of Maillane. He was virtually the Comte de Provence. He was undoubtedly the most influential figure in the South of France and perhaps the most beloved. He hobnobbed with the mighty and

---

3. *L'En-Avant de Frédéric Mistral* (Paris, 1931), p. 221.
4. Madame Darmesteter, in an essay in *The Contemporary Review*, vol. 62 (1892)

the celebrities of Europe, and they went to Maillane to pay him homage. Yet he still remained with the poor. He refused to use a horse and trap to get to and from the station at Graveson and took the local bus like the people, as later he refused to buy a motor car when his weekly visits to Arles would have made it a boon. Neither honors nor public adulation could blunt his honesty and sincerity. He was always himself in any company, and he could always be relied upon to speak his mind without prejudice, even if everybody did not like what he said. He had the deep moral earnestness of the Hebrew prophets and of Dante. His simplicity of life was reflected in such things as the frugality of his meals, the austerity of his bedroom and his walks and conversations with the peasants in the fields. "If you can talk with crowds and keep your virtue, Or walk with Kings—nor lose the common touch." This, in Kipling's words, he could do, and did.

His circle of friends was ever widening, and scattered through his works and letters are allusions to people, many of them august, who cannot be referred to in detail here. In *Nerto* alone one finds that Book One is dedicated to the Queen of Rumania (who wrote under the name of Carmen Sylva), Book Two to the Countess of Toulouse-Lautrec, and Books Six and Seven to the Countess of Gasparin and the Venetian Marchioness Maria Licer respectively. Among his greatest friends was Madame Adrien Dumas, better known as *Dono Andriano* and sometimes called "the Swallow of Nîmes." For about twenty-five years Mistral was the king of her *salon* in the beautiful house on the Rue Briçonnet of Nîmes. Another was Léon de Berluc-Pérussis, poet, savant and economist, with whom Mistral corresponded to such an extent that a selection of close to two hundred of their letters has been published. Two distinguished literary figures who drifted within Mistral's orbit were Maurice Barrès and Charles Maurras. Both were to cause him discomfort at times. Barrès defended the traditions of French nationalism and the glories of military service, but in his cult of the soil and of ancestor worship he was also a defender of regionalism, seeing almost eye to eye with Mistral on matters of regional culture and tradition. Maurras abandoned his native Provence for Paris, where he became a member of the Félibrige, and he received encouragement from Mistral, but later his thought and influence were distorted by his doctrine of exclusive nationalism and his fanatical direction (with Léon Daudet) of the newspaper *L'Action française*. Originally to be regarded as a spiritual heir of Mistral, he soon proved an obstacle and a nuisance (and his subsequent downfall in our own time seems to have been inevitable).

It was in 1894, on October 14, that Mistral attended a great bullfight in the Roman arena of Nîmes. This was more significant than may at first appear since bullfighting, both the Spanish *mise à mort* and the milder version of the Midi, had been officially banned since 1873. Mistral was thus defying the French government and espousing yet another local cause, despite the fact that he personally did not like the Spanish bullfight and had protested against the introduction of a Spanish bull strain into the *manades* (twenty years earlier he had written a witty piece in the *Armana* called "The Protest of the Bulls of the Camargue"). Yet here he was allowing himself to be summoned with the rest for illegal bullfighting, paying the fine of sixteen francs. No wonder then that when he entered the arena the crowd of twenty thousand rose up and shouted "Mistral!"

It has been remarked that the people of Provence and Languedoc "honour their God and their river with the same name," and Mistral in the notes to his *Poem of the Rhône* recalls that the Provençal word *Rouan*, a word which signifies the bull, is also an emblematic word for the Rhône. There comes a line in this poem: "And let the Bull-Rhône bellow in Rouanesso!" It may indeed be true, as President Doumergue once said in the French Chamber, that "In the south, the passion for bullfighting is more deeply rooted than in Spain itself." Doumergue knew, for he was a son of the Midi and as a Cabinet Minister had himself entered the bullring at Aigues-Vives. The cult of the bull in Provence, the Mithraic cult, had existed from time immemorial. On the façade of the church of Caveirac a sculptured bull altar recalls the Mithraic sacrifice made in honor of the Emperor in the third century, and the church of Les Saintes Maries itself is said to have been a center of this cult—though there is little or no evidence, it is maintained that the gypsies still practise a watered-down Mithraic rite in the crypt, for the letting of blood is characteristic of gypsy ceremonies. Elsewhere in many churches of the South altar motifs and decorations are rich in Mithraic symbolism, with horses drawing the chariot of the sun and bulls drawing that of the moon.

In the Marquis Folco de Baroncelli-Javon, one of Mistral's most staunch Félibres of the second generation (and now assistant editor of L'Aioli), the Mithraic cult had a champion. He held that the savage black bull of the Camargue was the same which in the time of Xenophon had haunted the plains of Thessaly. More, it was the descendant of that great Asiatic breed which had swept westward until, following the course of the Rhone, it settled in the delta of the great river. No one did more to make Les Saintes-Maries and the Camargue, the land of fire and water, the center of the bull cult. At one time indeed he attempted to sacrifice a bull to Mithra in the crypt of the church of Les Saintes and was pained when the curé refused to allow it. But there was far more than that to Baroncelli. He was a fine poet and a scholar, he was a gardian and a manadier, he was a champion of oppressed minorities and he was a mystic. He was sprung from that Florentine patrician family whose memorial chapel is to be seen in the Franciscan church of Santa Croce at Florence, a family one of whom had taken part in the assassination of Giuliano de Medici and had been compelled to flee to Provence. Thus it was that the young Marquis (born in Aix in 1869) had inherited the fine Gothic Palais du Roure with the sculptured oak branches of Pope Julius II over the door that still stands in Avignon. The life of an aristocrat in the Papal city was not for him, however, and as soon as he had become of age he had retired to an island in the Rhône near Avignon, there to breed bulls, to write poetry and to devote himself to Mistral and the Cause of Provence. The Félibrige came to number many aristocrats within its ranks, but none (certainly not Bonaparte-Wyse, who was an elegant gentleman to his fingertips) remotely resembled this strange modern Don Quixote.

Baroncelli has written some powerful and haunting poems, among them *Babali* and *Lou Blad de luno* (*The Lunar Corn*), and he has paid tribute to his own deity Pan, the bull, in *Le Taureau*.

I am the Bull which, from Asia
To the forests of Liguria,
Has reigned in Joy, Art and Blood
Over the Mediterranean peoples.
My image adorns the temples of Assyria.
I have given my strength to the Romans.

I am Apis, I am the Minotaur
. . . .
I have known the Centaurs
And I have been the god Mithra.

          *   *   *

People of the South, above all you young men
Keep your trust in the Bull,
I promise you, I will be your talisman and your shield,

Incarnate me in thy faith, believe truly
That I am Apis; I will be Prouvènco for thee,
I will be the Pare and the Sanglier.[5]

The poem recalls the gathering of the gypsies at Les Saintes and the mysteries of fire and water in the church crypt, and it pays tribute to the *gardians* and their almost sacred vocation. "I have lain with the seed of Ariane," Baroncelli goes on, and he concludes with the sentiment that the ideal taurine *cocarde* is "the seven-rayed Star" (i.e. of Santo Estello). "I have brought it to Maillane, for thy Poet, on my brow." This poem provides the basis of the epilogue in *Les Bestiaires* by Henri de Montherlant, Baroncelli's nephew. In this remarkable novel, which is virtually a treatise on tauromachy, Baroncelli figures as the High Priest of the Cult of Mithra. Another young Félibre, José d'Arbaud, who was to become Baroncelli's son-in-law, was also a devotee of the Camargue and was almost equally imbued with bull fever. His poems *Rêverie d'un Gardian, Chant des Fers* (a tribute to the *gardian's* trident) and *Le Laurier d'Arles* are still recited at fêtes and banquets of the cowboys, and his novel *La Bête du Vaccarès* (like the poems, originally written in Provençal), a story of a *gardian's* encounter with the last surviving demi-god of Provence, half-bull, half-man, is essentially Provençal-Greek in spirit and gives some explanation of the quasi-mystical feeling which the bull cult arouses. Yet another taurine classic is *Sangar*, by Jean Toussaint Samat, which was dedicated to Baroncelli.

Indeed Arles and the Camargue became more and more the center of Mistral's world. As Marcel Coulon put it, "Although Maillane was nearer to Avignon than Arles, the latter town was the focal point of his earth. Mistral was an Arlésien and never an

5. *Prouvènço* (Baroncelli's own bull), the *Pare* and the *Sanglier* were the last three great bull deities of the Midi.

Avignonnais. *Mirèio*, his first work and his masterpiece, the poem which drew most from himself and from his early memories, was enacted in Arles' soil. Arles itself found in it that which had appeared to the eyes of the child Mistral, for it was from the lips of a child that Mistral paid it homage." It was therefore not surprising that when Mistral planned his great Palais du Félibrige he planned it for Arles. It had a modest beginning in 1896 when Mistral hired the first floor of the Chamber of Commerce building, the old College of the Oratorians, with its mournful grey seventeenth-century façade with shuttered windows, opposite which stands an old church that has now become a garage. He declared his aims in *L'Aiòli*. As the *Tresor dóu Félibrige* enshrined the words of the Provençal language, so this Museon Arlaten would enshrine the visible and material forms of Provençal life. It was to be "a museum of the living life and people of Arles." Though not until he had won the Nobel Prize some eight years later was he able to fulfill this dream.

BOOK FOUR

Pavane

He hath skill in language;
And knowledge is in him, root, flower and fruit . . .

THOMAS LOVELL BEDDOES

Man with his burning soul
Has but an hour of breath
To build a ship of truth
In which his soul may sail . . .

JOHN MASEFIELD

These eyes, that now are dimmed with death's black veil,
Have been as piercing as the midday sun,
To search the secret treasons of the world:

SHAKESPEARE

And like a new-born spirit did he pass
Through the green evening quiet into the sun.

KEATS

CHAPTER 10

Poem of the Rhone

THE SPEED with which well-loved and familiar things change and
even completely disappear in our own lifetime can be galling
enough. If Mistral had seen an ancient way of life perish by the
eve of the Great War, how much more accelerated has been the
change over the past half-century—the spoliation of vast areas of
Provence, the vulgarization of the Côte d'Azur, the introduction
of ricefields into the Camargue, and above all the transformation
of the Rhône Valley. Between Montelimar and Orange the valley
today lies a wilderness of mud and cement as the Donzère-Mon-
dragon project and its satellites push on to completion. This, the
largest hydro-electric installation in Western Europe, is changing
the shape and course of the Rhône in no uncertain fashion, in-
volving dams, a twenty-mile canal and a lock with the world record drop of eighty feet, while more and more dams are to be built
along the entire course of the river. The farmers of the Rhône
Valley will benefit by this irrigation, but much is inevitably lost
in the process.

We live in a world of flux. Mistral too had seen great changes
on the Rhône. In his boyhood Arles itself, like Avignon, Beaucaire
and Tarascon, was the center of a substantial *entrepôt* trade, and
it was even busier than the others since it was there that merchan-

167

dise coming down the river was transferred to sea-going vessels plying between Genoa and Barcelona, and, vice versa, transferred from the Mediterranean ships to the river craft for the voyage up to Lyons. In 1850, on the eve of its downfall, the fleet of Arles consisted of some 150 boats, employing some 4,000 people, almost a quarter of the population of the town. The boat-building quarter was at Trinquetaille (where the young Félibres danced on a bridge of boats), where it had been since pre-Greek times, and most of the sailors lived in the Roquette quarter, where they held their fêtes. The river was then crowded not only with the new steamboats but with the even then disappearing barges dragged upstream by teams of up to forty horses in rows of four abreast, which made the journey from Arles to Lyons in about a month, a somewhat hazardous voyage along a swift river treacherous with islets, rocks and shifting sandbanks, while the bridge of Saint Esprit with its narrow arches was always a risky encounter.

It was in 1828, two years before Mistral was born, that the first steamboat appeared, making the same voyage in two days. Stendhal made his journey to Provence on such a boat in 1837, and Dickens, in his *Pictures from Italy*, writing of his voyage from Lyons to Marseilles in 1845 referred to "a very dirty vessel full of merchandise, and with only three or four other passengers." But both steam paddle boats and barges were themselves to give way to tugs, and these in turn to motorcraft. The railways too played a great part in changing the life of the river, and altogether the old life of the Rhône and its sailors was utterly vanquished, far more completely than the old life of the soil in *Mirèio*, which even today can still be identified.

Mistral naturally took all this to heart, and his own early memories of the river were reinforced by the stories he had heard from his father and from old friends, especially a knowledgeable wood-cutter and his old servant Jean Roussière, who as a youth of twenty had been in charge of eighty stallions drawing six boats along the river and had known all the inns and landladies, the tufted islands and polished rocks, the tributaries and streams, the wooden jetties, the roads and fords along the Rhône Valley. It was now, in 1897, that Mistral's tribute to the mighty river appeared. It was to be his last major poem. *Lou Pouèmo dóu Rose* (*The Poem of the Rhône*) is the story in twelve cantos of a barge train coming down the Rhône in the last days of horse navigation and, symbolically, of its clash with the first of the steam paddle boats. Interwoven with this brilliant evocation of the old life of the river and its sudden destruction is the legend of a girl who fell in love with the Drac, the fairy tale prince who was also an aqueous monster living on the bed of the river. Without any preliminaries the narrative opens on a note of action:

> *From Lyons in the rosy-tinted dawn*
> *The watermen, masters of the Rhône, depart.*
> *A robust and mighty band of men, these Condrillots,*
> *Their faces gilded to the hue of bronze*
> *By the sun's heat and the water's glare.*

The barge train is assembled, and the final preparations are made for departure. The lusty mariners fill the air with their oaths as they finish off their meal, the hunks of meat swilled down with the red wine. Their lives and their homes are simply described. Such a train of boats usually consisted of up to ten craft, the leading vessel being that of the captain, which had a cabin in which he ate and slept. Here each barge is described, and the leading vessel is the *Caburle* and its master Apian, a mountain of a man with patriarchal grey locks and two big gold rings dangling from his ears. These skippers, like the pilots, had some social standing, and indeed a skipper like Apian was a 'Monsieur.' Such men were known as the 'Emperors,' and until 1944 (when it was destroyed by bombing) the principal inn of Tarascon was the Hôtel des Empereurs. The teams of horses are roped together and now draw the vessels away, and the captain's cry goes up, "Steady, turn her downstream now. *Royaume! Empire!* Prow upstream! Pull on the towropes!" In the language of the river men *Royaume* and *Empire* are steering terms designating starboard and port respectively going downstream, and vice versa on the way upstream, a terminology having its origin in the days when the Rhône was the boundary between the Kingdom of France and the Holy Roman Empire. The river was long an artificial frontier. Apian recites the Lord's Prayer as he stands on the poop, and the convoy sets sail for Beaucaire.

> *The great river is panoplied with craft,*
> *Covering the long Rhône, a procession*
> *Of barques and ships of all sorts . . .*
> *How many are they! Some carry pointed*
> *Lateen sails and others square-rigged,*
> *Lighters from Arles, brigs from Marseilles,*
> *Tartanes of Genoa or of Leghorn,*
> *Aleppo brigantines and balancelles of Malaga,*
> *Naples and Majorca, English schooners, or*
> *From Havre-de-Grâce, the pig-snouts of*
> *Adge and Cette, the black trabacs of the*
> *Adriatic . . .*

Not only the shipping but the landmarks are all described in detail, and at times we are reminded of Mark Twain's *Life on the Mississippi.*

In the second canto the young Guihén or William, Prince of Orange and son of the King of Holland, boards Apian's boat at Vernaison. He is handsome, and his beard is the color of the yellow iris. He is perhaps a romantic, a wanderer in quest of an ideal symbolized by the Zwanenbloem or swan's flower of his own country. At Condrieu some of the boatmen meet their families, and here Mistral resorts to his old trick of describing their lives and customs and the technicalities of their calling. The *Caburle* now takes on board three Venetian women bound for the great fair at Beaucaire, and one of them sings a ballad which evokes in the Prince a memory of the barcarolles that softly drift on the waters of the Grand Canal. There ladies tell the Prince that their family has been living for generations upon the belief that their lost wealth is buried in Avignon, near the Palace of the Popes. The Prince admires them for their illusion:

> *And you do well, indeed, exceedingly well,*
> *Said the young sage; for what is life after all?*
> *If not a dream, a remote semblance,*
> *An illusion on the glistening waters,*
> *Which fades away before our eyes*
> *Like the play of a mirror which dazzles us . . .*

In the fifth canto L'Angloro makes her appearance. She is the eldest daughter of a Rhône pilot who lives with her family near the junction of the Ardèche and the Rhône, and she is nicknamed L'Agloro (the lizard) because she is always out in the sun. She is standing on the shore washing out the gold dust from the sands brought down by the Ardèche, which provides her with pocket money. The crew of the *Caburle* chaff her and the goodnatured banter goes backwards and forwards. But she is a strange quiet girl who disdains all the possible suitors among the watermen. She has her own dream. Here the note of fantasy enters into the narrative. For L'Angloro is in love with the Drac, the mysterious divinity of the river, the serpent-like creature who could take human form and decoy mortal women to his underwater lair. She had seen him and almost yielded to him one hot summer night when bathing. When he had slipped away from her he had left her a flowering rush as a token.

He was splendid and slim as a lamprey, turning in the water-whorls while his green eyes pierced you from his whiteness. His long green hair, silky as seaweed, flowed about his head in the waves. It is said that his fingers and toes are webbed like a flamingo in the Camargue, and that there are two fins at his back as transparent as blue lace.

When the barge train reaches Malatra L'Angloro comes aboard with her father, the pilot. She meets the Prince and looks into his green eyes as into the eyes of her predestined lover, for there is mutual recognition. "I recognize thee," cries the Prince, as he offers her a flowering rush, "Flower of the Rhône that blooms upon the wave." And, pale and trembling, she answers him. "I recognize thee, O Dra, whom I have seen with that same flowering rush beneath the water."

Meanwhile the boats have entered Provence by the Pont Saint Esprit, with its score of arches "set like a coronet upon the Rhône," the gateway to the land of love. Smollet[1] referred to this bridge on his journey of 1763, when he observed that travellers from Lyons

> . . . glide down this river with great velocity, passing a great number of towns and villages on each side where they find ordinaries every day at dinner and supper. In good weather there is no danger in this method of travelling, till you come to the Pont St. Esprit, where the stream runs through the arches with such rapidity that the boat is sometimes overset. . . The boats that go up the river are drawn against the stream by oxen, which swim through one of the arches of

1. *Travels through France and Italy* (London, 1766).

172

this bridge, the driver sitting between the horns of the foremost beast.

The distracting quality of the river in its grey adagio moods now dominates all the crews and even affects the idyll of the lovers. This melancholy is intensified as L'Angloro tells the company of the oracle at the fountain of Tourne, of the prophecy of the old witch, who declared that the carvings on the Mithraic monument there foretold disaster to the river and the doom of the sailors, while even the Drac himself would be driven from the river forever. And the boatmen are uneasy, for they have heard rumors of strange new vessels breathing fire and steam that can sail the river without horses. A later incident, when the whistle of a ship carrying convicts to Toulon shatters the silence, is regarded as an evil omen. Orange is left behind, and in the City of the Popes there is a diversion in the form of a treasure hunt organized by the Venetian women. Ultimately skipper Apian brings his convoy to Beaucaire, opposite castled Tarascon which perhaps reminds L'Angloro of those other lovers Aucassin and Nicolette.

At Beaucaire the great annual fair is in full swing. It survives today in a much less virile form, but in those days it was another Nijni-Novgorod, having developed from the old Phoenician market, to which the spices of the Indies, the silks of China, the ivory of the Congo and the furs of the Arctic found their way. Many people of many races jostled before the booths on the banks of the Rhône, and upon the broad river rode ships laden with merchandise from every Mediterranean port. The fair and all its wares are described in detail, and here the lovers wander "in a protracted intermezzo slightly reminiscent of the fair-scene in Gottfried Keller's *Romeo und Julia auf dem Dorfe,* where the lovers, Sali and Vrenchen, are likewise depicted before they are touched by the shadow of tragedy; for romantic love can only be fulfilled by death, by the Liebestod."[2]

Now the Condrillots make ready for the return voyage to Lyons; the team of horses is harnessed to the *Caburle*. At dinner before they set out Prince Guihén speaks bravely of the river and its traditions, and though the company feels instinctively that their way of life is threatened they drink to the Rhône and the life-giving sun. The sun sinks over Nîmes and its last rays burnish the castle of Tarascon. With the dawn the voyage upstream begins, and Apian asks the blessing of God and the Virgin. The carters leading their steaming horses take up the prayer. Did Apian make his invocation standing at the ship's rails or in the little chapel or oratory which was built at the stern end of the boat? Mounted on the poop there was usually a large ornate crucifix of wood, the *Croix d'Equipage*, often carved with the instruments of the Passion.[3]

As the last canto opens the mistral wind is hurtling down the valley. L'Angloro and Guihén talk of the marriage they will celebrate at the foot of the Mithraic monument at the *font de Tourne*, for the Drac-Prince cannot be married as others are. On this mystic note Mistral refers to the Mithraic shrines of Bourg, Lyons and Arles and the blood cult of the bull, vaguely recalling Baroncelli's wish to sacrifice a bull to Mithra in the church of Les Saintes. This also suggests that the Drac is in some way related to the cult of Mithra. It is a bizarre marriage that is envisaged here, yet L'Angloro in her anxiety to preserve the sanctity and the sacrament of marriage calls upon Saint Nicholas, whose chapel on the bridge of Saint Esprit is now passed, to bestow his blessing. But it is too late, and the turn of events now takes a dual symbolism, for the convoy has only just negotiated the bridge when the sight

2. Rob Lyle, *Mistral*, p. 51
3. There is an excellent example in the Museon Arlaten, Arles.

of a huge black monster belching smoke and flame appears suddenly round a bend of the river. It is the first of the paddle steamers. Captain Apian refuses to give way to this intruder. "The Rhône is ours!" he cries. The steamer crashes into the line of boats, sinking them and dragging the horses into the water. Everything is lost—the entire fleet of vessels and the teams of superb stallions, but the Condrillots themselves are spared and, now safe upon the river bank, Apian vows to say a Mass to Saint Nicholas for their miraculous escape.

L'Angloro and her Prince, however, are missing. Either they are lost or the Drac-Prince has at last carried off the mortal woman to his watery lair. Apian in defying Progress paid the price. Did L'Angloro pay a greater price for her defiance of Christian morality? The issue is deliberately left vague. This is perhaps the most agnostic in flavor of Mistral's major poems, yet he brings in the religious tradition to purify and rejuvenate the primitive epic. Folklore is used as symbolism. It has been said that the Drac was an *esprit diabolique*, but does this mean something other than the Devil himself? Is this the old conception of the demon-lover, or is the Drac nothing more nor less than an illusion of *L'Angloro*, who has identified it with Prince Guihén? By the use of this device Mistral is once again able to introduce the local survival of witchcraft, the spirit world and the personification of the river as far as its deification in the cult of Mithra.

As a narrative poem this is probably Mistral's best work, and it is certainly the easiest to read since it is constructed in *laisses* or short sections of unrhymed eleven-syllable verses. In *Lou Pouèmo dou Rose* we hear the voice of a mighty river, we feel its moods, its oppressiveness and its menace, its tranquility and its benediction, and all its pulsating life, and if the poem is the embodiment of a great river it is also a tribute to a race of men who have vanished with their craft.

In the year of the Rhône poem Daudet died; it was a year which
had seen the production of yet another opera based on *L'Arlésienne*, this time to the music of Cilea, produced in Milan. Daudet,
the great showman who had laughed at Provence, had gone. Yet
he had loved Provence, and though he had written little in Provençal the greater part of his work had been inspired by Provence.
And was he not an honorary member of the Félibrige? Mistral
must have felt his loss keenly. The public mind, however, was at
this time almost exclusively engrossed in the Dreyfus case, the
trial of the Jewish army officer accused of treason, of espionage
on behalf of Germany, which was creating bitter partisanship
even within the Félibrige. Mistral, like Daudet and Barrès, supported the verdict of France and the Court, and he was not to be
swayed by Zola's petition in the following year. He then wrote to
Paul Mariéton, pointing out that some people had tried, unsuc-
cessfully, to convert him, and continuing, "This Zola is unlucky
in every way, but if France and the Republic are not to die of nau-
sea God must be merciful." Which suggests that he was at least
discomforted by the affair. Mistral cannot be blamed when so
many were wrong, and though Dreyfus was later to be vindi-
cated all the evidence was against him at this time. It was a year
in which Mistral had his own troubles, for he was now compelled
to bring the publication of *L'Aiòli* to an end.

The spirit of partisanship so easily evoked within the Félibrige
by the Dreyfus case was as easily created by other matters. Some
of the stories of this period are, however, so dubious that they
must be dismissed as apocryphal. Félix Gras, dying in 1901,
wished a civil burial, but Mistral refused to appear at the inter-
ment if the rites were not conducted by the clergy. Consequently,
so it is said, he persuaded the Gras family to give the dead *capoulié* a religious burial. The fact is, however, that the related
Gras and Roumanille families, the latter staunch Catholics, had

their own bonds and their own agreements and had no need of any persuasion from Mistral. Again, it was at the burial of Gras, so it is said, that the Félibre Albert Tournier approached Mistral with the request that the latter ally himself with the Freemasons —it is difficult to believe that Tournier knew his master so little.

More significant, and this time perfectly true, was Mistral's opposition to his friend Albert Arnaveille, Catholic and Royalist, as *Capoulié* in succession to Gras. Instead, he favored the Protestant Pierre Dévoluy. Some of Mistral's gestures in support of his declared policy of neutrality seem sometimes to be quixotic. He wrote to Dévoluy, "The fact that you are a Huguenot is all the more reason why you should accept. It is entirely right and good for it to be seen that the Félibrige is bound neither to a religious denomination nor to a political party." A little later, on April 12, 1902, Mistral wrote Dévoluy a touching letter:

> During these last few days there has arrived in crowded Maillane a girl, a servant in the home of one of my aunts, who for me is the incarnation of Mirèio . . . radiant with youth, with grace, with innocence and with pure beauty. And do you know where she comes from? She comes from Châtillon-en-Dois, your own country. . . She is Protestant and her name is Rose! One can only think that the Countess of Die has sent to us the very pattern of the flower of the Félibrige and the accomplished pattern of the *Capoulié* elect.

There was nothing bigoted about Mistral, he was generous to a fault.

Meanwhile, Folco de Baroncelli, freed from his duties on the suspended *L'Aiòli*, was absorbing himself more and more in the life of the Camargue. More, he had adopted the races of Atlantis and had become the champion of the gypsies, and now in the aftermath of the Boer War—an interlude which alienated the affections of the Félibrige against the British—he was offering hospitality to Boer refugees. Just as he held that the gypsies of the western Mediterranean were the descendants of prehistoric man, driven into persecution by the Iberians, so he held that the Red Indians, likewise persecuted in North America, were of the same stock. So the redskin too came to receive his hospitality and Buffalo Bill brought over the redskin chief Sitting Bull and his family. The chief of the Sioux, Philip Blue Shield, visited him at his *mas*, and some of these refugees, among them the Indian poet Michawago, remained at Les Sainte Maries until they died.

If the Sioux were Baroncelli's 'red brothers' so were the gypsies, who made him an honorary *Crayi* or King of the Gypsies, and whose baptisms, marriages, funerals and ritual feasts he attended. He was a man of strange ideas and impulses. For him the gypsies, Red Indians, Egyptians and Basques were all descendants of the inhabitants of Atlantis, of aboriginal Stone Age tribes who still visited their ancestral shrine at Les Saintes, where their backdoor saint, Sara, was really, so he held, a priestess of the Mithraic cult and if not a Romanichal almost certainly an Egyptian. Similarly he held that the superb wild white horses of the Camargue were descended from the remote Solutrean breed. To this revived horse and bull cult the gypsies quickly and naturally adapted themselves, for the letting of blood so characteristic of gypsy rites was continued in the *mise à mort*.

Baroncelli was not merely a *gardian* living the rough life of Véran in *Mirèio*, for he was the leader of the *gardians* and he was Prior of the *Confrérie des Gardians* founded under the patronage of Saint George in 1513. And now he founded the *Nacioun Gardiano* or National Guard, which, allied in purpose to the Confraternity of Guardians, sought to bind the cattlemen together and to preserve their historic rites and traditions, as he revived the old tournaments and created several variations on the *jeu des oranges* and the *tourbillon des roses*. This splendid body always turns out to accompany religious processions and is itself proof —if any were needed—that Baroncelli was a practicing Christian even if an unorthodox one, vaguely equating what has been called "the religion of blood, caste and military imperialism" (Mithraism) with the spirit of the Catholic Church with its Faith, Hope and Charity.

Baroncelli then had brought the Félibrige from the Café Voltaire of Paris back to the salt marsh of the Camargue, back to the land of Mirèio. His lonely figure in faded colored shirt and moleskin riding breeches, with a red and white sash around his waist and a battered sombrero on his bearded head, would be seen riding behind his bulls amid the reeds and tamarisks. His white *cabane* partly built of reeds, the Mas dou l'Amarèu near Les Saintes, stood facing the sun, and on a wall were written the words *Que Dieus renda la terra als sieus fizels amans.*[4] (God gives the earth to his faithful friends). On the walls were hung the bull fighter's sword and *muleta*, some pictures of bulls and horses, autographed portraits of Sioux chiefs, and in the midst of these simple things were gathered a few luxuries from his Avignon palace, including some eighteenth-century furniture. Loaded guns rested in a corner against the walls. Here he would prepare his own food, for he was an excellent cook, and would go out to break some branches of peppermint wood to scent the tea. The silence was broken only by the galloping hooves of horses and bulls and by the distant soughing of the sea. On the horizon a flaming pink cloud would drift down to earth as the flamingoes settled in the delta.

While Baroncelli was founding the *Nacioun Gardiano*, Mistral was establishing the *Festo Vierginenco* (1903). Mistral had long

4. From the 13th century *Chanson de la croisade.*

been concerned for the preservation of the costume of Arles—he wrote an article on *Lou coustume Arlaten* in the *Armana* of 1884 —and the *Festo Vierginenco* was an annual fête designed to promote the wearing of this dress, when those girls who wore it were presented with a diploma designed by Léo Lelée. The local costume had, however, undergone modifications since Julien Reattu and Antoine Raspal, the leaders of an Arles school of painting in the eighteenth century, had painted those stiff portraits of Arlésiennes which are to be seen in the town's museums. In fact it now conformed to the mode prevailing under Napoleon III, and it has changed hardly if at all since then. Mirèio was the sister of the Tanagras of Athens and Smyrna and like them she had acquired the art of piling up an immense length of hair, as she had learned the antique art of draping her body.

Léo Lelée, who died only in 1947, was a Mistralian and a fine draughtsman with a touch of genius, and he was virtually a social historian since his work provides a unique record of an elegant community that is no more, though it survived the Great War. In his drawings, pastels and oils we see the women of Arles in their homes and on the boulevards, crowding down the steps of Saint Trophime, dancing alfresco and carrying Japanese lanterns at a fête. Except for variations in the patterns and colors of the dresses the tall stately figures are almost indistinguishable one from another. All wear, by day, the velvet *ruban* with floating ribbons, the tight-fitting *eso* or bodice with jewelled *chapelle* of gauze and embroidered muslin, the *jupe* or skirt, the goffered lace collar or *foulard*, and the bright *fichu*. And, by night, a slight variation in the substitution of a rich lace headband for the *ruban* and a large cape in place of the *fichu*, though in cool weather the *enveloppe* or *manteau* with its peacock-bright floral figuring was invariably worn.

Mistral, of course, was at the back of all this, prompting and satirizing those women who abandoned the local costume for the latest Paris modes. In Paris, indeed, people began to laugh and make jokes about the "*Folies Arlésiennes.*" Despite the Grecian elements there is something decidedly oriental about these figures, and seen through the eyes of Lelée they have often a startling Japanese quality. They are highly stylized and they seem to glide through a dream world. Many of the pictures in fact so resemble ballet that one expects the prima ballerina to come on from the wings at any moment. Lelée's drawings inspired the somewhat garish frescoes which until a few years ago were to be seen in many Arles hotels and restaurants, where the diner was distracted by costume-pieces which had become more Japanese than ever. It was as though the Arles of the latter part of last century had been embalmed by Mistral and Daudet, Gounod and Bizet and Léo Lelée.

Yet this world of ritual and costume should be seen in true perspective. It was not an arty-crafty movement; it was not the resuscitated medievalism of a William Morris. Nor is it valid to compare the costume of the Arlésiennes to the frippery of the Morris-dancers at Stratford-on-Avon—one was a living tradition with continuity, an integral part of the local wardrobe, while the other is as spurious as the Druidic robes of the Gorsedd. Nothing indeed is more beautiful than the Provençal costume, but rarely now, unfortunately, do the young belles wear it outside the *fêtes folkloriques* and the *Festo Vierginenco*, occasions for bringing out the *galoubets* and *tambours*, the pipes and drums of Provence, equally despised by the "progressive" as "folklore." With what strategems of casuistry the "progressive" defend their own gods it is difficult to imagine when those gods are the epileptics of tin-pan alley and the racing track.

Half a century had now passed since that day at Font-Ségugne when "the Seven" had founded the Félibrige. It was May 21,

1904. A hundred Félibres and a thousand other people lunched alfresco in the groves of Font-Ségugne. It was a moving moment when Mistral, straight as an oak despite his seventy-four years, recited the nostalgic piece he had written for the occasion:

> *The Seven of Font-Ségugne—singing in*
> *our own tongue—we were like gods . . .*
> *The beautiful singers are dead, but their*
> *voices re-echo; the builders are dead, but the temple*
> *is built. . .*

The builders are dead. . . For of the seven Félibres, 'the gay Félibres of Provence,' only Mistral and Tavan were left. And a year later Tavan was to go, to be commemorated by a bust on the fountain of his native village Châteauneuf-de-Gadagne. Understandably then, this must have been a sad occasion for Mistral. Yet there was consolation enough in the growth of his organization and in the numerical strength of Félibres of the second and third generations. And now in this same year came one of the crowns of his life's work—the Nobel Prize for literature.

It was unfortunate—but significant—that when the first Nobel Prize for literature was about to be bestowed in 1901 one or more newspapers announced that the recipient was to be the great poet of Provence. Quite obviously his claims and merits had been pressed, but the prize was actually awarded to Sully Prudhomme, the French Parnassian poet and essayist. Some indignation was expressed that the Swedish academicians should have considered an honorable but by no means extraordinary poet to be more worthy than the epic and lyric poet who had honored an entire people and created an entire field of literature. Mistral, ever modest, took all this in his stride. Amends were made three years later when he was awarded the prize, but even then there was an element of surprise and dissatisfaction for in fact he received only a *demi-prix*, sharing it with José Echegaray y Eizaguirre, the Spanish popular dramatist. The latter was indeed a talented and versatile man, a distinguished engineer, a successful financier and economist, and a former Minister of Education and then of Finance at Madrid. Nobel had decreed that the prize should go to a person "who shall have produced in the field of literature the most distinguished work of an idealistic tendency."[5] It seems strange then that half of the prize should go to the Spanish playwright whose plays were of romantic or Calderón techniques, plays which were vague and woolly and phantasmagorial. Despite the compromise, however, Mistral benefited to the tune of 100,000 gold francs (a great deal of money in 1904) and a great deal of publicity which revealed him to the world at large. It also made possible the Museon Arlaten as we know it today.

In a letter of September of this year Paul Mariéton compares the "radiant old age" of Mistral with that of "the sage of Weimar" (other writers have noted an affinity between Mistral and Goethe in their pious youth, their dazzling use of the twilight hours of later years, and their deep spiritual life which lacked the outward manifestations of practicing Christians). Mariéton, however, notes a difference in the religious sentiment that gladdens the home of our poet, and he refers to a significant incident. "He has been struck more than I dare think by the unexpected and heart-rending death of the Félibre (Auguste) Marin. The anticlerical campaign is very bad in Provence. You have read in the newspapers of the recent incident at Maillane during the traditional procession (Notre-Dame de Grâce, August 28), the arrival of the hussars, etc. Briefly, Mistral, very grieved, has begun to think about death; he has been to Avignon to buy a crucifix with

5. Later it was found impossible to apply Nobel's condition in judging between single works, and the prize was awarded in consideration of the author's total output.

183

which to sanctify his house. . ... He has never been a free thinker, but his Goethism is linked to the faith of his fathers."

The year, as always, was filled with work and engagements which presumably did something to alleviate the spiritual malaise which seems to have come upon him. Added to his public roles was a new one as honorary president of a Mutual Benefit or Provident Society which was now set up in Maillane, presumably in consequence of the tragic death of Marin. About this time too he was encouraging Cécile Sauvage, the young poetess, daughter of a schoolmaster living in Provence, to write.[6] His influence probably bore fruit in many ways, and one may suppose that his teaching on tradition and the regional arts inspired local peasant craftsmen—as late as 1900 a Maillane shepherd, Jean Blanc, carved the Twelve Apostles with Christ and the Virgin on a winder (this is now in the Museon Arlaten).

In 1906 his book of memoirs *Moun Espelido, Memori e Raconte* (translated into French as *Mes Origines, Mémoires et Récitatifs*) was published. This, perhaps the most well loved of all Mistral's works, is a European classic and one of the most fascinating of autobiographies, but, unfortunately, it covers Mistral's life only up to the triumphant publication of *Mirèio* in 1859. Yet Mistral was right in feeling that it rounded off an epoch and that it marked the end of his youth, and there is no doubt that it covers the most colorful episodes of his infancy and young manhood, introducing us to his parents, the life of the farm and the entire rural community, the arts and traditions of his Rhodanie, the scenes of his formulative years, the first Félibres and their exploits. As far as it goes it is perfect, and Mistral was too great an artist not to realize that to go further might have marred it. Its quality of warmth and humor, of sincerity and conviction, place it poles

6. Her poems of maternal love and others were published posthumously, *Oeuvres de Cecile Sauvage* (1929).

apart from such seedy confessions as those of Rousseau, and in
its rural tranquility it is perhaps reminiscent of those Memoirs
which the earlier writer Marmontel wrote for his children in his
old age. It is hardly necessary to point out that any portrait of
Mistral must rely almost entirely for the years 1830-59 on this
absorbing and revealing work. Mistral wrote it in the twilight of
his years, and it is a magical world that he evokes, colored with
nostalgia perhaps, yet sane, robust and noble.

CHAPTER 11

The Last Harvest

EARLY IN 1906 Mistral was casting about for more ambitious premises for his Museon Arlaten. He had several old Arles mansions in view, but the most noble, spacious and in every way suitable building was the Hôtel de Laval-Castellane. This splendid patrician house in which the Gothic yet lingered was one of the earliest Renaissance palaces in the Midi. In the eighteenth century the Jesuits acquired it and converted it into a college, building beside it a chapel which today is part of the Musée Lapidaire and houses early examples of Christian art. In 1906 this Hôtel de Laval still housed the Jesuit College, but in view of the declining number of students there and the approaching completion of a new large school in the town Mistral began negotiations for its purchase. It was a lengthly business in which no less a person than Aristide Briand (later he too was to share a Nobel Prize, for peace) had a hand and finally made it possible. The Jesuit college would be transferred to the new school, and the Hôtel de Laval would be restored. A great deal of money was necessary for all this, and Mistral's ultimate aims were so ambitious that even the Swedish crowns of his Nobel nest egg would have to be implemented. His friend Jean Ajalbert having written some propaganda, presumably of a begging nature, in the *Siècle* and elsewhere, Mistral wrote thanking him for these 'New Year gifts,' adding that 'I still have need for your "Open Sesame!"' The world was invited to contribute. Mistral had thought of writing to Rothschild, but in the event he wrote to another Croesus, Pierpont Morgan, who did not reply. But the great industrial houses of the Midi, among them Vermouth Noilly-Prat, came forward.

It was over three years before the Hôtel de Laval was finally adapted to its new role. During the restoration the remains of a Roman building were revealed in the courtyard. Every Thursday Mistral made his weekly visit to Arles, as he did for many years. He would drink an absinthe in the Café Brusque and would lunch with friends in the Forum or the Hôtel des Hommes. In the winter of 1908-09 he contracted phlebitis and was ill enough to close his door for three months against all comers, even his friends. Fortunately he recovered in time for the great celebrations arranged to mark the *Cinquantenaire* of the publication of *Mirèio*. Just before this, however, there was the annual Santo Estello banquet held on April 7, 1909 at Saint Gilles. The choice of Saint Gilles in this significant year came as a surprise and created much argument and ill-feeling within the Félibrige, and at the banquet there were such strong words that the proceedings developed into a brawl in which the peasant-poet Laforet (he was a wagoner) punched Paul Mariéton in the jaw and knocked some of his teeth out.

It went without question that the three-day celebrations for the fiftieth anniversary of *Mirèio*, beginning on May 29, would be held in Arles, though there were some who favored Maillane and some Avignonnais who made the obvious demands. The series of fetes and ceremonies was on a scale that few men of genius, certainly few poets, have received in their lifetime—and fewer still have been present at the unveiling of their own statues and taken the leading parts in their own apotheosis. The statue was also the subject of much controversy, and some favored a bust of Mirèio or Calendau on the heights of Les Baux, that Acropolis of ancient Provence. By the end of the previous year, however, the celebrations committee had commissioned the well-known sculptor, Théodore Rivière, to execute a full-length figure of Mistral. The large statue in aqueous green bronze depicts the poet in late middle age, wearing his characteristic wide-brimmed hat and carrying his walking stick, with his cloak slung over his left arm. The statue was mounted on a pedestal in the Place du Forum and later enclosed with railings in the form of *gardians'* tridents. Mistral took all this with his usual sangfroid, but there is little doubt that he was somewhat embarrassed. As he remarked to Charles Roux, "I shan't dare to walk about Arles any more. People will say, 'Look, here's the bronze come off its pedestal.' "

On the opening day the patriarchal poet—he was now one year off four-score—drove over from Maillane with his wife and the servant 'Marie-du-Poète.' Arles was so crowded that Mistral must have had difficulty in reaching the Place du Forum. Special places were set aside for the illustrious, for the representatives from many countries and for the committee. The French government was represented, and the French Academy (for which Mistral had declined to become a candidate) sent the Vicomte de Vogüé. The Queen of Rumania sent Prince Cantacuzene. The Queen of Portugal, President Theodore Roosevelt (who had written Mistral a congratulatory letter in 1904) and the government of Sweden were also represented. There were distinguished scholars, philologists and professors from all over Europe, among them the Germans Tobler, Morf, Appel, Stengel, Foerster and Volmöller, the Dutch Salverda de Grave, the Italians Crescini, Novatis and De Lellis, the Austrian Cornu and the Swedish Wahlund. British and Americans seem to have been conspicuous by their absence. Particularly conspicuous was the mistral wind which was persisting into summer and was now howling through the decorated streets of the town, ripping to shreds some of the painted scenery for the opera *Mireille* in the arena. Perhaps, however, it was not entirely unwelcome to Mistral, who, having learned his Nostradamus at his mother's knee, recognized the wind's sudden advent as a tribute to himself.

From the wind-swept rostrum in the Place du Forum speaker after speaker paid glowing tribute to the poet. Indeed it was an occasion which brought out all the hyperbole of the South, one speaker solemnly asserting that the publication of *Mirèio* was "not only a literary event, but also an historical one of greater importance for civilization than the outcome of a battle or the destiny of an empire." Yet this was perhaps more than a *galéjade,* a boast of the Midi, and for that insatiable audience in the packed square it was little less than truth. As Ford Madox Ford aptly remarked, "To find yourself in harmony with the soul of Provence you have to be of a type that will not be pained when someone says that Mistral was a greater poet than Goethe—or that the Maries, after the Crucifixion, came to and settled in the country around Tarascon. Indulgent Provence has no vested interests, and there illusions do not matter."[1]

After all this and the unveiling of his own statue Mistral himself had to mount the rostrum. It was a poignant moment and the old man had tears in his eyes. What could he say in such circumstances? The crowd must have wondered as it became silent and waited. But Mistral was equal to the occasion. He thanked them simply for all the nice things they had said about him—and then he recited the opening lines, the Invocation, of *Mirèio.* The incident was as epic as his poetry. "We seemed to be seeing, in the market place of some Ionian town, Homer himself dominating the

---

1. *Provence* (London, 1938).

people by the majesty of his gestures and his words," wrote one witness.

This deification of a living poet may seem strange and even in doubtful taste to a people which reserves its acclaim until its poets are safely tucked away in the vaults of Westminster Abbey. And there may seem something a little histrionic in the celebrations which followed, for in addition to the unveiling of the statue and the official opening of the Museon Arlaten there was a Bal Mireille, all the women of course sporting local costume, there were farandoles and traditional songs, displays by the *gardians,* and the final culminating performance of Gounod's opera *Mireille* in the flag-spangled Roman arena. A painting by José Belon in the Museon Arlaten shows the multitudes rising to greet the poet as he entered the arena to take his seat. Certainly Mistral must have been proud and touched by all this, but was it not for his 'Rhodanie,' for Provence? Back in his austere monkish bedroom at Maillane that night did he perhaps live in retrospect his life's work and consider it well done?

But it was not yet over. In the following year there appeared his Provençal translation of Genesis, which, as we have seen, he had begun as far back as 1878, publishing a chapter each Christmas in the *Armana* under various pseudonyms. The complete work was published in Paris and it included a French translation by J. J. Brousson. It is strange that Mistral, a Catholic, should consider it necessary to write such a work, and equally strange that he should allow it to be published without the official *Imprimatur* of the Church. This law of the Church did not in fact apply to newspapers and periodicals and thus not to the *Armana.* The Genesis translation had, however, been vetted by the Félibre-priest Père Xavier de Fourvière, the young Norbertine of Frigolet and author of the Provençal-French dictionary *Pichot Tresor,* who had in his sermons actually cited at length chapters of Mistral's translation as they had appeared in the *Armana.* No doubt Mistral considered this enough, yet Cardinal de Cabrières, Bishop of Montpellier, had now to intervene to save him from censure.

It cannot be held that Mistral had any intention of writing a religious work, for he wished only to show the eternal life of the soil, the unchanging pattern of the pastoral life over the centuries and the affinity between the patriarchal life of Genesis and that of his own boyhood in Provence. The work is remarkable for its choice of words and its range of popular expressions, denoting once again, as in the *Trésor*, his gifts as a philologist. At the head of the book and under a photograph of the author appears verse XXI. 14. "And Abraham rose up early in the morning, and took bread, and a bottle of water, and gave it unto Hagar, putting it on her shoulder, and the child, and sent her away . . .' There is of course a slight variation in the Provençal and French versions of this. But why this choice? It is one of the many little problems which Mistralians have been unable to solve. Léon Teissier suggests that it expresses Mistral's regret that he was childless, or, again, that it recalls the departure of the young Mistral and his mother (the biblical Ruth) from the Mas dóu Juge and the sadness of parting. The title of the work carries the qualification *Translated from the Vulgate*, and Chapter XIX bears a heading indicating that it was translated from the Latin of Saint Jerome. Without doubt, then, Mistral translated his Genesis directly from the Latin, but it is no less evident that he also made use of French translations. Brousson's French text does not follow Mistral's Provençal, and indeed there seems to have been no reason for its inclusion. Jean-Jacques Brousson was a friend of Champion, the Paris editor of the work, and he had recently been raised to the archbishopric of Toulouse by the Félibre Monsiegneur Germain and was a specialist in scriptural studies as well as a keen reader of the *Armana*. It would seem, then, that Brousson was pushed into the Genesis project and that Mistral had little say in the matter.

The year saw some abatement in anticlerical activity in France, but the Freemasons invited Mistral to the Capitole to be crowned with the laurel of Petrarch, an enterprise which somewhat resembled the rationalist celebrations then going on at Tréguier in honor of Renan. To such invitations Mistral replied declining the honor and intimating that his own convictions and activities were in opposition. Indeed he now complained that certain people were trying to parade him as a curiosity, as a tourist *spectacle.* "I have become part of the tour; I am classed with the Arena and the Alyscamps." Cardinal de Cabrières seems to have been pleased by Mistral's cold response to the *coup du Capitole,* and he was responsible for drawing the attention of the Pope, Pius X, to *Nerto* and the Ode to the Immaculate Conception. The response of the Holy Father was to send the poet a gold medal and a signed letter of blessing addressed to 'our dear and very illustrious son.' The old man and his wife received it on their knees.

According to Maurice Barrès, each time that Pope Pius met Cardinal de Cabrières he asked him, "And Mistral, does he take the sacrament at Easter? I shall not die in peace if he does not."[2] One likes to believe that such a spark of affection existed between the two men, between the Pontiff, *Ignis Ardens,* the Burning Fire, and the no less patriarchal poet. Pius X (canonized in 1954), born Giuseppe Sarto, was a humble and saintly man who, however, abandoned the conciliatory policy of his predecessor toward the French Republic, making inevitable the separation of Church and State, which was finally brought about in 1905, and he defended the faith against 'modernist' interpretations, notably in his brilliant but then much-abused Encyclical *Pascendi.*

In 1912 Mistral brought out his last volume of lyrics *Lis Oulivado* or *The Olive Gathering.* As the olive gathering was the last harvest of the year in Provence so this was Mistral's last offering.

2. Léon Teissier, *op. cit.,* p. 109.

It is colored perhaps with a tinge of melancholy, with the intro-
spection of old age and the counsel of a wisdom at once serene
and resigned. There is a touch of pathos in the opening dedication, for he knew he was drawing to the end of his earthly labor.

> Lou tèms que se refrejo e la mar que salivo,
> Tout me dis que l'ivèr es arriba pèr iéu,
> E quo fau, lèu e lèu, acampa mis òulivo
> E n'oufri l'òli vierge a l'autar dòu bon Diéu.
> (The weather turns cold and the sea is rough, for me
> winter is here and I must gather my olives and offer the
> virgin oil at the altar of God.)

There are some fine poems here. Brèu de Sagesso (A little Wisdom) is in part a humorous translation from Pascal, but there
appear the lines "If life appears too paltry then let your eyes be
dazzled with the stars of night," lines full of ambiguity, perhaps
symbolic of greater reality and eternity, perhaps a mystic allusion
to his own star of Santo-Estello. There is Evo (Eve), a song of
physical beauty, Mount Toumbèu, a sonnet on his own tomb, and
Lou Parangoun (The Archetype). Dated on his birthday, September 8, in 1906, at the height of anticlerical frenzy and violated
and rifled churches, the last is sometimes held to be another declaration of his religious faith, but there can be little doubt that
the faith asserted here is his faith in Provence, in the Cause. "I
have locked my faith in the watch-tower of an old castle in Provence. . ." The Archetype, in fact, is Provence itself, seen now
in retrospect as a lofty ideal but perhaps no more than a dream,
an illusion. "My faith is but a dream . . . but still a dream that
seems veiled in gold." There is still much of the laughing philosopher, and if the old man has made his compromise with life and
with all those forces which threaten the things that are dear to
him he yet seeks to find the living faith under the veil of illusion.

The history and pageantry of Provence pass before his eyes, and then, sadly but inevitably, comes the decline. But wait, 'Santo Estello in the empyrean height' has performed a miracle and Provence flowers again, is reborn in Mirèio. Despite all, faith, at last, is not illusion and has its reward.

Another poem, *Mirage*, dated February, 1907, is about the *jongleur* Cercamon who has become a Benedictine monk. But the flesh pursues him into the monastery as the temptations of his youth return in the images of women that assail him toward the middle of the day, the time of accidie or acedia, the most dangerous hours of the monastic life. Cercamon makes humble confession. "My son," says the good prior of the convent, "calm your remorse. The years of your youth cannot return; your penance is made." For in truth it was not his faults but his youth that Cercamon regretted. Here Mistral in theology is for once the cousin of Dante, as he often is in poetry.

In August of 1912 Mistral was invited to become honorary prior of the Pénitents Blancs in Montpellier. He accepted—he may have felt that he could do no other, remembering his dead Pénitent friends Aubanel and Jules Giéra, and the history of the lost house of Pénitents Blancs in Maillane—but his letter does not contain a word of piety and refers only to history, literature and memories. "In memory and veneration of this institution, once extremely popular in the Midi, and which, at Montpellier, has as its director and patron His Eminence Cardinal de Cabrières, my illustrious friend and contemporary, I receive then with gratitude this testimony of sympathy which you have offered to me in his name." The Montpellier church of the Pénitents was and remains a charmingly decorated building of the seventeenth century, rich in carved floral motifs, with panelled and painted walls and ceilings and gilded festoons hanging above the altar, and the confraternity now set up on the church entrance a marble plaque bearing the opening quatrain of Mistral's ode *A La Raço Latino*.

Mistral may have felt justified then in asking, in the following year, for some small statues of Pénitents for his collection in the Museon Arlaten, but in so doing he seems to have provoked Cardinal de Cabrières, who was still trying to persuade Mistral to return to orthodoxy and who perhaps considered a museum no fit place for objects of piety. Mistral eventually got his *figurines de pénitents*, but meanwhile he was in trouble with his old and eminent friend (they were exactly the same age). The Cardinal had asked (it would be truer to say insisted) that Mistral as honorary prior should accompany a delegation of Pénitents to the celebrations in Arles marking the sixteenth centenary of the Emperor Constantine. Mistral was obviously reluctant and he weighed carefully every word of his reply. "If my health permits me, for at our age it is prudent not to make hard and fast plans, I shall be happy to go with you to Arles and to take part in the commemoration." The letter then went on to touch on historical considerations, and it was accompanied by this short note: 'For weighty enough reasons and for reasons concerning my work in the Félibrige, I beg you not to give this letter publicity. Keep it, if you wish, in the archives of the corporation but do not publish it . . . until after my death.'[3] Mistral managed to salve his conscience in reckoning with God, but he had not reckoned with the Cardinal. And so he took his place in the Arles gathering and was present at some regrettable political demonstrations, which was just what he had wished to avoid.

It was indeed a year of embarrassing situations in the political field. President Poincaré, in the first year of his presidency, visited the Midi and made special journeys to see Mistral and the distinguished entomologist Henri Fabre who lived at Sérignan. Now the President was denounced for not going to church, and the women

3. Léon Teissier *op. cit.*

of Maillane remained all the day of his visit in their morning working clothes, *en catalane*, while the municipal councillors refused to see him. Mistral was very angry about this, and (since he was himself a councillor) he sent for the official register and wrote in it these words:

> Acò's la Signaturo dou Presidènt de la Republico Ramoun Poincaré, lou jour que venquè à Maiano vèire lou felibre Maianen, 11 d'òutobre 1913. F. Mistral.

He held his rancour, however, for Charles Maurras and the *Action Française*, who had stirred up trouble and enmity. Later Mistral complained, "It was to Provence that the President paid his tribute. Why have they brought politics into it?"

Time was running out, and Mistral knew it. We have seen how, nearly a decade ago, he bought a crucifix. And now in the summer of 1913 he bought another. One account[4] tells how, carrying this new crucifix, he met the abbé Aurouze, another Félibre, in the streets of Avignon and addressed him thus: "Look how beautiful this is. . . Are you surprised, my little one, to see Mistral carrying the good Lord in his hand, like this, in the crowded streets? You see, when one grows old one must think of everything. When I am ready to go and the Captain comes to sign my papers for the great voyage, I would have this in my room, on the *commode*, well in evidence. . ."

According to another version, however, it was Térèse Boissière whom Mistral encountered in Avignon. Térèse offered to carry the little parcel which the poet carried.

"No, no, it is not heavy."

"But, dear Master. . ."

"No, no, inquisitive; you want to know what is in the parcel—ah, well, just guess. . ."

4. Léon Teissier *op. cit.*, p. 112.

"Master. . ."

"You are unable to find out—so I will tell you. There is no crucifix in my room at Maillane. I have always intended to buy one. . . eh, bien, that is what I am carrying. . . You understand I say to myself that Mistral cannot die and meet le Bon Dieu without a crucifix."[5]

Had he then bought two crucifixes? The first was probably for the wall of the drawing room, and the second with its little pedestal was for the last rites. There is today such a crucifix as the latter in Mistral's house on the *commode* in his room, but it must be admitted, despite the fact that he had a pious wife, that the house was far from being encumbered with objects of piety. The acquisition of these crucifixes cannot truly be regarded as a manifestation of contrition, for despite his lack of orthodoxy he had little enough to be contrite about. And if, like Dante, he had thought for a while that moral perfection was to be acquired by the unaided efforts of human reason, such an ambitious mental approach had soon given way to a humbler and deeper realization of Christianity.

A fortnight or so before he died, in March of 1914, Mistral wrote a piece for a priest-Félibre in which he saluted Notre Dame de France, the patron of Puy. The next day Monsignor Borel, rector of Notre Dame de la Garde, the basilica of Our Lady of Sorrows in Marseilles, asked for a song of praise for his own patron. Mistral replied that there was sufficient to choose from in all his published work, so the rector submitted a postcard bearing five verses from the poem *Mère de Dieu*, a choice with which Mistral agreed. The poem concerned had appeared in *Lis Isclo d'Or*, and in it Marseilles is referred to as "the ardent and joyous city" which "never closes its eyes before the splendour of the Mother of God."

There was a new bell in the church of Maillane, and on the

5. Jean Ajalbert *op. cit.*, p. 177.

bronze the *abbé* Celse, with Mistral's approval, had had engraved the poet's two quatrains beginning *Campano, voues de Diéu* (*Bells, voice of God.* . .), followed by the date and signature, *Maiano, 19 de mars, 1914, F. Mistral.* In the late afternoon of Wednesday, March 18 (the day before the dedication ceremony), the *abbé* went to see the old poet about the arrangements. Mistral was out, though he shortly returned with his wife from a country walk. Upon hearing from the servant Marie-du-Poète of the *abbé's* call, Mistral went straight to the church to inspect the bell. It was about five o'clock, the mistral wind was blowing and it had turned very cold. When he removed his hat on the threshold of the icy church he shivered and he said, "It is not warm here." But he was in a good humor and he stood joking with his old friend Daillan, a neighbor from infancy. On his return he said to his wife, "I am going to be ill." On the following day Madame Mistral made it known that he had too bad a cold to take part in the ceremony of dedicating the bell. No one took it very seriously, and by Sunday the *abbé* Celse had not called. When reproached he said, "Oh, a cold is nothing to bother about."

But it was bronchitis, dangerous enough at eighty-three years of age. On the Sunday, about midday, he took to his bed, though it is also said that he had taken to bed from the first day. He grew suddenly worse. Early on Wednesday, the 25th, Marie-du-Poète having drawn the curtains, Mistral said to her,

"Marie, what day is it?"

"It is Wednesday, Master."

"Then it will be Wednesday all day."

A light-hearted sally, a popular expression, proving that Mistral was one of the people until the end, but words now strangely and sadly significant. Marie took him a bowl of foaming milk to abate the fever. For Mistral even now did not realize how ill he was; nor did his wife—when she did it was too late, and seeing his troubled eyes she said, "Commend yourself to the Saintes Maries." Mistral did so, and his words were like an echo from the past: "*Li Santo! Li Santo!*" He was to say nothing more. Like his Mirèio he was to die in the arms of the Maries.

Doctor Terras was quickly summoned. The *abbé* Celse was lunching with a neighbor when Marie-du-Poète called in some agitation, "Madame Mistral begs you to come at once—the Poet is very ill." The old man was breathing heavily with pain and was unable to press his lips to the crucifix; since he could not speak he could not be confessed. The *curé* gave him conditional absolution and then he administered the last rites. Mistral's large eyes were still open and his lips moved, and it was only when the priest had given him extreme unction that his eyes closed. Without suffering, he drew his last breath. As with his own *Meissounié*, the harvest was ripe and the Harvester had come to gather it in.

It was an hour after midday. *La Daiano*, the new bell in the church of Maillane, which had first rung two days earlier for passing knell for a dead woman, now rang out for the second time, this time for its own poet. Soon all Maillane was mourning. *Mistral est mort!* It was the time of the mulberry picking. *Cantas, cantas, magnanarello. . .* Were the young girls in the mulberry trees too grieved now to sing, or were they of another generation oblivious to the passing of their patriarch? Did the old shepherds pause to cross themselves as they drove their flocks on the hillside? Did the *gardians* in the dreary wastes of the Camargue rein in their horses and raise their tridents in silent salute?

The *abbé* Celse at once sent a telegram to Cardinal Merry del Val, who replied with the condolences of Pope Pius. A letter from Cardinal de Cabrières to the newspaper *L'Eclair* confirmed Mistral's resolve before illness overtook him to return to orthodox religious practice and the sacraments:

In announcing to our readers the sad news of the sudden death of the great Provençal poet Frédéric Mistral, we wish to state that it was agreed with him that I should go, on Monday next, to hear his confession. He has received, in full knowledge I am sure, the letter in which, conforming to the wishes of his friend Doctor Cassin, expressed to me in the name of Mistral himself, I promised to visit him and congratulated him on being ready to reconcile his faith with the holy practices of religion.

I go to say Mass for him with confidence, for I do not doubt that, resolved to humble himself by the free confession of his faults, he had at heart the sincere regret, the contrition . . . necessary for God's forgiveness. And who can doubt that God would ever delay to forgive the repentant?[6]

He was buried in the little Maillane churchyard beneath the monument which was ready waiting for him, since he had had it built to a design of his own choice some years back. It is in fact a reproduction of the small Renaissance pavilion near Les Baux, popularly known as Queen Joanna's Pavilion, which naturally had appealed to Mistral, though he must have been aware that local tradition had confused *La Reino Jano* with Jeanne de Quiqeran, Baroness of Les Baux, the real instigator of the monument. This Pavilion of Eternity, as Mistral called his tomb, is imposing enough, a light cupola supported on slender columns forming a circular colonnade. Mistral seems to have toyed with the idea of enriching the monument with sculptured heads of Arlésiennes (as on his house) and a mask of his dog *Pan-Perdut*, for, as he remarked, "We must not forget those who have inspired us." His architect may have discouraged this, for the pavilion is of classical simplicity and has little or no enrichment beyond the Félibrean star of Santo Estello. Nor does the poet's name appear,

6. Léon Teissier *op. cit.*, p. 119.

and this spartan anonymity is relieved only by a Latin epitaph. As early as All Saints Day, 1907 he had written the poem on his tomb, *Moun Toumbèu*, later published in *Lis Oulivado*. It is not in the humble Christian tradition of his epitaph, but it recalls, for the last time, his laughing philosophy:

Before me I can see the close and the white cupola where like the snails I shall curl up in the shade. The last effort of our pride to escape devouring time, which today or tomorrow fast fades to a long oblivion.

And when the people ask of Jan di Figo or Jan di Guèto or some other, "What is that dome?" they will answer, "It is the Poet's tomb."

"He fashioned songs for a beautiful Provençal girl they called Mirèio; there are as many of them as mosquitoes in the Camargue,

Scattered about everywhere. . . But he stayed in Maillane, and there are old fellows here who remember seeing him walking along the footpaths."

Then a day will come when they'll say, "They made him King of Provence, but his name survives only in the chirping of the brown crickets."

And then, quite puzzled and unable to explain, they will say, "It must be the tomb of a magician, for the monument has on it the image of a star with seven rays."

The funeral orations were over. But there was yet one more, eloquent, curious and quite unexpected, for the occasion was the marriage of Mistral's grandniece Josephine Mistral to Albert

Bertrand in the chapel of the Institut Fénelon at Nîmes on April
18. The words were spoken by Père Janvier, who, to use a meta-
phor of Léon Teissier, "twined mortuary drapings in the white
veil of a young bride."

"Mademoiselle, mon cher Albert. .. .

We had hoped that all Maillane would attend this religious
ceremony, that its sun would gild this day with its rays, that
its cypresses and plane-trees would protect with their shade
your nuptial procession, that its new bell, still vibrant with
those graces received at its dedication, would sing in your
honour one of its first hymns and gather in its joy all the
echoes of the plain. We had hoped above all that Mistral
would stretch out his patriarchal hands to touch your brows
in blessing and draw from his incomparable lyre one of those
glorious strophes which edify as much as they charm. But
Providence, sovereign mistress of our destinies, has opened
a tomb, an immense grief which envelops in its funeral folds
all the Latin peoples. *Cecidit flos!* Provence has lost its flower. God has carried off the greatest, the most popular, the
most well-loved of his poets to enter, I trust, into the celestial choirs of His court. Mistral is dead! He has died at the
hour when he promised to lead you to the altar, to assist at
the exchange of your vows, to entrust to you the treasury
of ideas and traditions to which he had dedicated his life
and genius. A first blow had delayed the realization of your
dreams. This second misfortune throws a veil over a ceremony which should have been all radiance.

Meanwhile, the will of God commands you to give your-
selves up to hope, to look towards the future in order that you
may not break faith with the past.

Wounded in the flank, the old harvester of *Lis Isclo d'Or*
begged his young companions to honour him by continuing
with their task and tying up more golden ears of corn than

he could himself. Those who have departed from you make the same plea. . . The sacrament wills that you shall love one another undividedly and forever. But the grace of marriage itself needs to be nourished. . . When death knocks for you in your turn it does not break the bonds which hold you, for your love is stronger than that which would come between you, dissolving the mists of the Crau as day dissolves the darkness of night. Here in this crowded sanctuary, where friendship has offered you a gracious refuge, and in Maillane where they dream of you in an alloy of tears and happy expectation. . . all raise their voices and ask God's blessing upon you. . . Mistral, having reached the night of his long and glorious day, invoked the good Saints, sovereigns of Provence; invoke them also in the morning of your life; they will be, I am sure, the invisible but powerful protectors of your hearth until the end."[7]

When one speaks of the sincerity of Mistral one does not ask whether he was sincere but in what manner he was sincere. Some little attempt has been made in the foregoing pages to reconcile his politics with his faith, his beliefs with his religion, but any amount of investigation and analysis would still leave him a somewhat enigmatic figure. Genius is not to be measured by the common yardstick. Mistral had the dualism of Dante. Giovanni Papini in his biography of the Florentine observes:

Dante is undoubtedly a Christian, although not a perfect Christian—and who except the saints could pretend to be a perfect Christian?—and he is a Catholic Christian, an enemy of heresy; yet he preserves in his heart a deep affection for the pagan philosophers. . . Dante does not choose between the Church and the Empire. He accepts the Church provided it reforms. He desires the Empire provided it fulfils its func-

7. Léon Teissier op. cit., p. 121.

tion. He does not wish that the Emperor should become the master of the Pope, nor that the Pope should usurp the mission of the Emperor. And he brings together these two great powers, which had been for so long a time in opposition, and equalizes them in a higher purpose which transcends them both—the service of suffering humanity, the triumph of peace.

These words might almost have been written of Mistral.

Professor Etienne Gilson makes the fascinating speculation[8] that many of the great artists, had they not become artists, might have been saints, and he cites Dante, Baudelaire and Wagner. Mistral too may be regarded as an example of the poet who not only displays these two tendencies but is aware of them. There have of course been poets who hated orthodox religion and yet were more religious, more concerned with sanctity, than many practicing Christians. Rilke was such a one. Where Mistral is enigmatic, however, is that while every line he wrote acquiesced in the teaching of the Church and even endorsed it he stopped short within sight of the confessional and the host.

A man of many facets, if he was an inspired dreamer he was also an inspired thinker and a national leader. "A synthesis of local forces," he not only recreated a language and made a large slice of France vocal, but he also made the civilized world aware of its heritage and of the blight which threatened it.

"... What one notices particularly in Mistral's remarks," wrote Léon Daudet,[9]

are their depth, the symmetry of his point of view, the broadness of his vision, as befits a descendant of men who have looked along on wide fields and star-filled skies. So I re-

8. *Pétrarque et sa Muse.* Deneke Lecture (London, 1946).
9. *Souvenirs des milieux littéraires, politiques, artistiques et medicaux.* 1914-21. The above translation is by Rob Lyle, *op. cit.* pp. 46-47.

member him down the vista of thirty years or more, judging equitably men and events, singing the praises of his
province, and elaborating methodically, unremittingly his
idea for her reconstruction, on a scale more grand than even
his friends have realized. . . In Paris, Mistral was criticized. . .
Since then it has been proved that Mistral's ideas were anything but chimeric, that they were sternly practical. The attitude of the Master of Maillane stimulated and encouraged
the superb resistance of Alsace and Lorraine; those who up-
held the heroic soul of Alsace, her hopes and customs, did
so with the weapons that Mistral had forged. . . Incompara-
bly the most gifted of all our poets—including Hugo—Frédéric
Mistral is familiar with those formulas that link the State
and the Word and add to the strength of both. . . Those shel-
ters which he constructed and of which he sang will, in days
to come, afford a refuge for defeated nations seeking to escape the yoke of their oppressors.

And this is what Eugène Lautier had to say:

Men of France, of the north, of the middle, of the Midi, exalt
Frédéric Mistral without fear of contradiction. We are not
alone. All the Latin family of Europe and America proclaim
its legitimate pride of race and of the services rendered to
civilization. But I wish here to salute the non-Latin peoples
who have recognized in Frédéric Mistral one of the classical
singers (vates) of humanity. Frédéric Mistral, poet of man
and of nature, is universal. His genius reaches out not only
to our own province but to all frontiers. . .[10]

With the Comtesse de Noailles, all France could now acclaim
him:

> *Ton coeur enveloppe ta race*
> *Et ton pays descend de toi.*

10. Jean Ajalbert, *op. cit.*, p. 207.

CHAPTER 12

Aftermath

A FEW MONTHS after the death of Mistral Europe was stunned by the assassination at Sarajevo. When the Emperor Francis Joseph asked for the Papal blessing upon the 'punitive expedition' against Serbia, Pius X promptly refused. "I bless peace," he answered, "not war." Within a month, on the day that the German army entered Brussels, he died of a broken heart. The cataclysmic disaster which followed did not invalidate the work and ideas of either Pius or Mistral, both far-seeing visionaries, but the thunder of the guns along the Marne ended an epoch and broke up the old world.

When the holocaust was over men turned once again to garnering and preserving all that was best in the past, all that which across the scorched shell-shattered years was now even more remote and in even greater danger of being lost forever. The founding of the *Ligia Romontscha* or Romansch League in Switzerland in 1919 almost certainly owed much, however indirectly, to the work of the Félibrige, especially since the Romansch tongue has affinities with old French and Provençal. The league was founded to preserve and develop Romansch language and culture in the canton of Grisons, where it quickly ousted the encroaching German. One of the leading lights in this movement, Pater Maurus

Carnot (1865-1935), the Swiss Benedictine monk, was certainly inspired by Mistral, for he encouraged the study and cultivation of Romansch poetry and wrote folk tales and dramas with romantic historical background and lyrics which, like those of Mistral, were expressive of his faith in God, his native country and the unspoiled life of the peasant.

The high hopes of the Catalans in their contact with the Félibrige were somewhat dashed by a long period of prohibition, though despite this Catalan lyric poetry blossomed fully. Even today when the Franco régime bans most works in Catalan, as well as the teaching of Catalan in schools and universities and its use in official and public places, the movement continues. The Bretons have had similar troubles but they too were strengthened by Mistral's example, though they have failed to establish a standard literary language, and the four major dialects of the country have tended to keep Breton literature on a provincial basis, an almost exactly similar problem to that which Mistral and Roumanille had managed to overcome.

Old *Maman* Roumanille, Joseph's widow, was not only still alive but at ninety years of age was correcting proofs for the *Armana Prouvençau*. She was now stricken with her first illness and she complained, "Doctor, you are not going to let me die in the prime of life!" Yet Térèse Boissière, her daughter, was dead at fifty.

In 1920, when the world was busy erecting war memorials, the people of Rhodanie were putting up a statue of Mirèio in Les Saintes Maries. There is something inconsequential and unreal about such a gesture at this time, but there is something heroic too—France, suffering and bled of her sons, could still remember her poets and those who had inspired her. The statue, enclosed by iron tridents, was designed by Antonin Mercié and unveiled in the presence of Madame Mistral, and it depicts a peasant girl suffering from sunstroke, a dramatic figure with one hand raised to her aching head. Eight years later a statue of Mistral was set up in the garden of his house at Maillane. It did not arrive there without opposition and a miniature storm which blew up in the newspapers, where it was referred to as a 'turnip,' a piece of barley sugar, an affront to the memory of the poet. Most of the Félibres and other friends of Mistral seem to have been against it, but Madame Mistral defended it and replied in the newspaper *Comoedia* to an attack by Gabriel Boissy. In loyalty to her husband she could have done little else, since the sculptor Achard had received the poet's approval and consent years earlier.

It must be admitted, however, that this monument is not too happily realized. Set in the now congested garden, at the foot of a *micocoulier* or nettle-tree which Mistral himself had planted, the poet in wide-brimmed hat and long jacket, one hand in pocket and the other holding a jacket lapel, leans against a broken antique column. The Arles statue is a better one, though this too had been referred to as a *navet*. The pedestal bust of Mistral in the Rue de la République of Avignon, close to the ancestral palace of Baroncelli, is perhaps the most successful of them all. The work of Jean Pierre Gras, this too was unveiled by Madame Marie Frédéric Mistral. There are other memorials scattered about the Midi, like the bronze medallion of the poet on the castle walls in Saint Tropez, the inscription cut in the honeycombed rock above Petrarch's celebrated 'fountain' on the edge of Vaucluse, and the marble plaques cut with quotations from the poet displayed in the streets of Montpellier. In the Midi Mistral is as omnipresent as is Burns in Scotland.

We glanced earlier at other Félibrean memorials, among them those to Roumanille and Tavan. Now another went up on the windswept heights above Les Baux, a monument in a desert. This time it was the pedestal bust of Charloun Rieu, the laboring poet who wrote *Chants du Terroir (Songs of the Earth)* and the words of the Les Baux *pastorale*. He died in 1924, having existed toward the end on a meagre government pension awarded mainly through Mistral's good offices, though it may have been Rieu who received a sum which Mistral, out of his Swedish crowns, set aside for 'a poor Félibre.' In 1943 Folco de Baroncelli died, in 1947 Léo Lelée, and in 1950 José d'Arbaud.

About 1928 Baroncelli moved from the Mas dóu l'Amarèu to the new Mas dou Simbèu, which he had built, and in 1936 he married Angele Vernet, a "Queen of Arles." His happiness was short-lived. With the second World War came the German occupation and the burning down of his *cabane*. Baroncelli died shortly afterwards, probably of a broken heart. He was buried in Avignon, but it was said that his body would be brought back to the Camargue, to Les Saintes Maries, his spiritual home. There is today a tiny museum in Les Saintes, housed in an old towered building which was once the Hôtel de Ville, a strange collection of the stuffed fauna and dried flora of the Rhône delta, indifferent copies of Van Gogh's local paintings, Hollywood-like souvenirs of the Red Indian refugees and relics of the *gardians*. And among them is Baroncelli's saddle and the head of his celebrated bull *Prouvenço*. His *Nacioun Gardiano* still flourishes and has its headquarters here, and since his death the *gardians* have revived yet another old custom, attending in force and *à cheval* the Christmas Midnight Mass at Albaron. They still ride out into the painted desert where the haze over the lagoons is filled with mirages, with the *Fata Morgana*, where the flamingoes fall to earth like a cloud of pink cherry blossom, and the beaver lurks among the reeds and disturbs the mauve goose-foot. But the Camargue is changing, and tender green rice fields encroach ever further southward toward the Mediterranean.

In Arles the Hôtel Nord-Pinus,[1] where Mistral often lunched,

1. The proprietor, M. Bessier, formerly a clown of international repute, was not only a close friend of the Maquis but during the last war sheltered the British agents Odette and Peter Churchill in his hotel, the base of their underground operations.

has a memorial to the cowboy-Maquis in the form of a room named after him; it was the room in which he so often stayed. It is therefore not surprising to find tridents in the hotel hall, though this displaying of local relics may be distracting and suggest all the elements of a hysterical tourism. One restaurant displays stuffed flamingoes, and another until recently had preserved a series of frescoes by Lelée. Arles itself has declined into a somnolent backwater, roused only by the music of *galoubet* and *tambour* at *fêtes folkloriques*, by the coaches flashing between Marseille and Paris, and by the sudden volcanic outbursts of laborers sprawled in tipsy lethargy outside the *bistros*. The Boulevard des Lices, or one half of it, has been destroyed by commerce and vandalism, the little classical theatre is closed for the greater part of the year, and the rococo chapel of the Carmelites has turned Huguenot. Along the banks of the Rhône indiscriminate bombing has reduced to amorphous huddles what once were the Trinquetaille and Roquette quarters.

Yet Arles has preserved golden Saint Trophime and its Roman monuments intact, and among its proud boasts there is Mistral's Museon Arlaten, as intriguing a folk museum as may be found in Europe, and one of its prototypes (though the real pioneer in this field was Arthur Hazelius, who in 1873 opened the museum of Swedish life in Stockholm which has developed into the mammoth-scale Skansen). Such museums, with their cavernous galleries in which the human pulse has ceased to beat, may be as disturbing, perhaps as slightly comic, as a waxworks, but this is a valid testimony to a life lived in the time of our grandparents, and it provides an illuminating commentary on Mistral's life and work.

One enters by the Consistory, where are still held gatherings of the Félibrige, presided over by a figure of Mistral, a cast of Rivière's figure in the town. First there is a room of herbs and flowers, the walls hung with dried plants from a herbal collected by Alfred Mistral, and by each of these Mistral has written the Provençal name and its properties, factual or imagined (old women still scour the hills around Les Baux and bring herbs into Arles, to sell them on the steps of Saint Trophime). The staircase, of wrought ironwork by an Aix craftsman, is hung with the banners of the ancient guilds and the municipalities of Rhodanie and with those hung out during religious processions. Here too are copies of the '*Coupo Santo*' and the *pervenche* or emblatic flower of the Félibrige. Then comes the Gallery of Costume, in three sections from the time of Louis XV to our own day, followed by a large room devoted to the furniture of the region. What is called the Gallery of Rites, Customs and Legends houses collections illustrating myth, popular superstition and practices, including games, though there is a curious overlapping since the range includes not only documentaries on dances but religious images, *santons* and *crêches*, much of it the work of the local Carmelites. Another staircase is dedicated to souvenirs of Alphonse Daudet and his friendship with Mistral, and this leads to the picture galleries and the work of Léo Lelée (a glimpse of a lost elegant world) and to the collection of religious art, most of it from local or at least regional monasteries and churches.

The three most telling galleries are perhaps those of the Crafts of the Soil, the Rhône and the Mediterranean, and the Crau and the Camargue. The first and last of these illustrate *Mirèio*—the silkworm industry, the osier work from Vincèn's Vallabregues, the olive harvest, the mills—and the middle one illustrates *Lou Pouémo dóu Rose*, with models of early vessels and documentaries on the old maritime life. The Camargue gallery shows, in addition, the fauna and flora, the life and art of the shepherd and the operation of *transhumance*, as well as the life of the *gardian*, with a full-scale reproduction of a reed-built *cabane*, and the lore of the celebrated horses and bulls. In these galleries there is ample evidence of the relation existing between agriculture and craftsmanship in a highly civilized peasant community. Viewed in conjunction with a reading of the poems and the anthropological studies of Fernand Benoit, these exhibits form an admirable introduction to Provence.

Two other rooms are set out as living tableaux with wax figures, and they represent two events described earlier in these pages. The first, *La visite à l'accouchée*, depicts a mother lying in bed with her newborn child, while four other young women bring in their symbolic offerings, the egg, the roll of bread, the salt and the matchstick. The second, the Salle Calèndo, shows the Christmas Eve celebrations in a *mas*, the table ceremonially laid as we have noted, while the old patriarch with "calloused and trembling hand" pours wine on the Yule log, and the family, the *gardian* with his trident, and the farm are grouped about. A younger man who stands as though reciting verse is supposed to be the poet Charloun Rieu, reading from his *Chants du Terroir*.

There still remain rooms dedicated to the Revolution, the Castellane family, pottery, music (containing among other things the musical instruments belonging to the municipality of Maillane in 1793), and, not least of them all, that devoted to the Félibrige, to their portraits, literature and official pronouncements, and to Mistral himself, whose cradle and regional clothes are here preserved. Finally there is Mistral's own library and that of Paul Mariéton, or part of it, for when Mariéton, long secretary of the Félibrige, bequeathed his 30,000 volumes to that body a storm blew up between Arles and Avignon, rival capitals of the Empire of the Sun, and the books were ultimately divided between the Museon Arlaten and the Palais du Roure. The latter, Baroncelli's Avignon palace, also houses Félibrean correspondence and the original manuscript of *Mirèio*.

Avignon, as we have seen, has its share of monuments and memorials, and there are streets named after Frédéric Mistal, Joseph Roumanille, Folco de Baroncelli, Félix Gras and other Félibres. Joseph Roumanille's library still flourishes on the Rue Saint-Agricol, and an Aubanel is still printer to the Pope. The Château Chênes-Verts passed by marriage from the Séménows to the Bonaparte-Wyse family, and it was tenanted by the grandson of William Bonaparte-Wyse until the outbreak of the last war, when he joined the Free French Navy and afterwards farmed in Ireland. The house, appropriately enough, is today leased to the Municipality of Avignon as a hostel for students of Provençal. There are today in and about Provence some seventy-five societies and folkloric groups drawing their inspiration from the life and work of Mistral. One need mention only *Lou Flouriege* of Avignon, *La Miógrano* of Nîmes, the *Escolo mistralenco* of Arles, the *Escolo dis Aupiho* of Saint Rémy and the *Muso maianenco* of Maillane. The *Armana Prouvençau* is still published annually, alternatively in Avignon and Aix, and *Lou Félibrige*, the monthly report of that body, is published in Maillane and Aix.

In Maillane the flower-starred stream still flashes by the Mas dóu Juge, and the wheel of the water mill on the edge of the village still turns sluggishly. Mistral's hospitable Second Empire villa has become a museum, preserved exactly as he left it, each chair in place, each pipe upon its rack, its brown furniture and wallpapers fading, and the crowded animated study contrasting with the more poignant monkish bedrooms. It requires a rare flight of the imagination to overcome the feeling of mortality and decay common to such museum pieces. Mistral's spirit is more apt to be found in the sunlight, in the fields and farmlands glowing under the southern sun and the wide cypress-pointed Provençal sky, where the scent of thyme and lavender lingers on the air, and the

Alpilles smudge the horizon with a streak of lilac. And there in the lanes one may encounter Mirèio.

The cupola of a strange and elegant tomb peeps above the wall of the village cemetery, where the Poet, like the snails, has curled down for eternity.

> *Non nobis, domine, non nobis,*
> *Sed nomini tuo,*
> *Et Provinciae nostrae*
> *Da Gloriam.*

It was not for him, but for God, and to the glory of Provence, that the monument was raised. . . .

The Lion of Arles

A PORTRAIT OF MISTRAL
AND HIS CIRCLE

IN THE MID-NINETEENTH CENTURY, when
Frédéric Mistral gathered round him at Avignon the brilliant group that formed the
Félibrige with a view to stimulating inter-
est in the Provençal language, he had little
idea of the scope of the movement that then
began. The seven "gais félibres provençaux" brought about a revival of letters
that was to go hand in hand with the rehabilitation of the old language and make
the people of the south of France conscious
of their race and their heritage. As the principal poet of the group, Mistral was to produce his epic-romance *Miréio*, a story of
frustrated love in which Homeric grandeur
and the charm and simplicity of Theocritus are situated in the fair land of the valley
of the Rhône. In his verse the pagan, sensual world of romance is colored with a
delicate Christian mysticism and filled out
with the loftier and more sublime sentiments of Catholicism.

Mr. Edwards has here produced, however, no mere essay in literary history but a
vivid re-creation of a land, a people, a way

(continued on back flap)